I0803038

NO PRESIDENT

A Story Ballet of Enlightenment in Two Immoral Acts

by Kelly Copper + Pavol Liška

Nature Theater of Oklahoma

53 SP 49

December 2024
Brooklyn, NY

No President: A Story Ballet of Enlightenment in Two Immoral Acts
© Kelly Copper + Pavol Liška 2024
53rdstatepress.org

ISBN Number: 979-8989946150
Library of Congress Control Number: 2024946745

Book design: Kate Kremer
Cover image: Heinrich Brinkmöller-Becker/Rhurtriennale 2018
Cover design: w/d

Printed on recycled paper in the United States of America.

All rights reserved. Except for brief passages quoted in reviews, features, or essays, no part of this book may be reproduced without permission in writing from the publisher. This material, being fully protected under the Copyright Laws of the United States of America and all other countries of the Berne and Universal Copyright Conventions, is subject to a royalty. All rights, including but not limited to professional, amateur, recording, motion picture, recitation, lecturing, public reading, radio and television broadcasting, and the rights of translation into a foreign language, are expressly reserved. Particular emphasis is placed on the question of readings and all uses of this book by educational institutions, permission for which must be secured from the author.

No President is made possible by the New York State Council on the Arts with the support of the Office of the Governor and the New York State Legislature.

NO PRESIDENT

A Story Ballet of Enlightenment in Two Immoral Acts

by Kelly Copper + Pavol Liška
Nature Theater of Oklahoma

53rd State Press
Brooklyn, NY

CONTENTS

FOREWORD

No President was written as a ballet; it meant to be danced, not spoken.

And it was initially intended for a museum, not a theater space—the result of an erstwhile invitation by the Museum of Modern Art to make a performance for their 2018 exhibition Judson Dance Theater: The Work is Never Done.

Pavol and I had never before been invited to work within a museum, so it was an exciting proposition. We were intrigued by the idea of being in a "high art" space with different rules and expectations and were interested in the chance to engage with dance as well as the concept of "work."[1]

But for some reason, it wasn't meant to be. I can't remember what exactly happened—if the deadline for the exhibition was moved (or perhaps we scared them away when we said we wanted to rehearse with their security guards...) Whatever it was, this original encounter with the idea of playing in a museum with security guards was enough of a seed for us to start, and then (as it mostly does for us these days) this seed eventually blew across the Atlantic Ocean and fell onto fertile ground in Germany where the project was finally created with support from the Rhurtriennale and Dusseldorf Schauspielhaus.

---

1 Pavol had worked for several years as a security guard at the Metropolitan Museum of Art, and most of the security guards who worked with him were also artists who did this as a day job to have the time and income needed to pursue their artistic passions.

Additional (occult) ingredients for the steamy, fecund loam that this seed/show fell upon was the recent election of Donald Trump as President of the United States and the aftermath of his contested, misogynist, jingoistic rise to power. Add to that our abiding passion for Balanchine's *Agon*, silent film, slapstick, and Parisian Grand Guignol...and you get *No President*.

We were curious from the earliest stages of rehearsal to know how dance is "written" and how, in particular, "story" is enacted in so-called narrative ballet. In our initial research, we studied scripts for ballets such as *Swan Lake*, *Giselle*, et. al., and learned what exactly were the building blocks and traditions of classical ballet, so that we could create our own from scratch.

We burdened ourselves with a plot so intricate that we knew it would be difficult—if not impossible—to relate using movement only, and we began experiments to dance and stage the story, word by word, in our apartment. After only a few days we understood we all needed to be much more physically fit, and we began incorporating calisthenic exercises into our training—which then were added to the choreography, to became part of the show's formal vocabulary. In our ballet, *passe* and *rond de jambe* would exist on an even playing field with burpees and jumping jacks.

As we worked, we tried to set the movement to music from several iconic story ballets (*Swan Lake*, *Firebird*, *Le Sacre du Printemps*) eventually settling on *The Nutcracker*, which—though annoying—seemed to work best.

The company for *No President* originally consisted of five performers from our main company (two of whom were trained contemporary dancers, and the rest—not) plus a *corps de ballet* of local people consisting of dancers, students and dance lovers and amateurs from the Rhur Valley in Germany.

The various roles in the show (save for the narrator) are wordless and expressed only through movement. The characters of Mikey and Georgie are played by Ilan Bachrach and Bence Mazei, Tale Dolven plays Supervisor, and Gabel Eiben is Big Boss. The rest of the roles are flexibly played by the *corps de ballet* and by the company as needed. The pace of the staging is quick. The performers change in and out of costumes and characters from minute to minute—even sometimes second to second. In addition, they move all the furniture, transport more than 100 hand props on and off stage, and play inanimate objects and supernatural creatures such as: a freezer, a television, a couch, and a horde of surprise pandas (for "pandemonium erupts"), and Personal Demons.

The role of the narrator came to us relatively late in the show's creation process, born of necessity. At a certain point we had to concede that the story was just too unintelligible without some kind of textual overlay or explanation, and so decided to add an on-stage narrator (actor Robert M. Johanson) who would recite the entire script for the audience and guide them through the show. When we lost one of the actors who was playing the part of the Devil/Client, just a few weeks before opening, Rob also effectively took on this role. The result: an unreliable narrator/ trickster who moves in and out of the narrative himself, as Devil and Client, baiting Mikey, Georgie—and the audience, as needed.

o

When *No President* finally opened in Gladbeck, Germany in the fall 2018, America was mid-way through the Trump presidency. We continued to tour the piece in 2019 to additional theaters and festivals in Germany and had plans to finally open the show in New York at the NYU Skirball Center in November 2020, just before the next presidential election...

But, of course, this never happened. New York went on lockdown in March due to the COVID-19 pandemic, soon followed by the rest of the world, and theaters would not reopen for live audiences for almost a year. All travel was impossible, and international touring—which was our main source of income—effectively ceased.

Our last performances together as a company were in November 2019. We put the show into storage with barely any hope of reviving it again, until...2024.

Five years later.

Its been a strange mix of emotions to revisit this show again at this time in history. We've come through so much in the fugue-state interim, lived through the pandemic lockdown, the invasion of Ukraine, the overturning of Roe v. Wade, the withdrawal from Afghanistan, the Black Lives Matter protests—only to find ourselves on the precipice of yet another election with a suspiciously similar cast of characters.

Personally, now in particular, I find that Mikey and Georgie's paranoia and care about "the mysterious curtain"—and what's behind it—has, for me, a certain of piquant reality that it didn't have in 2019. I remember when the theaters first shut down, wondering if I would ever even see a theater curtain again—or have the chance to look upon the emptiness behind and wonder how to answer it.

Through the blackness and the haze, I do still believe it is "pregnant with possibility." And I'm grateful again to have the chance to be together—and to try.

—Kelly Copper, September 2024

ACT ONE

A squad of uniformed security guards huddles around their Supervisor. It's the beginning of the shift.

She gives a confusing pep talk, using her sex appeal to hold their undivided attention.

They jostle one another for a better vantage point, and listen lustfully, ogling her alabaster lineaments.

She encourages and belittles them at the same time, saying they can do this, they've trained hard, but also that they could never train hard enough, would never be good enough.

She's not only gorgeous, but funny too, and they giggle at her harsh words, then nod in agreement, and a wave of self-doubt washes over them. An insecure security guard is more effective than a cocky one.

One of the guards, Mikey, is in love with her. When she's around, through a magic trick he plays on his mind, the rest of the world first becomes hazy, then disappears completely.

It's just the two of them now in Mikey's micro-universe.

Time turns into sweet syrup, and they enact a classically romantic scene.

They're walking hand in hand through an imaginary flower garden.

Mikey stops, goes to kiss her cheek.

Supervisor pulls away, playing hard to get, only stoking his passion.

He skips to the other side and attempts another chaste kiss.

She scampers off, teasing, inviting him to chase, which he does with blithe delight.

She lets him catch her.

They embrace and stare into each other's eyes with desire.

But as their lips are about to meet, Mikey's paranoia conjures up her husband, the boss of the Agency they work for, whom she doesn't want to hurt.

Mikey understands, knows that cheating causes cancer. In his mind, she's moral perfection personified, an incarnation of carnal incorruptibility, and he loves her all the more.

Luckily, Big Boss is oblivious, crossing in the background on some faux-urgent business, and doesn't notice the trysting lovers.

Mikey and Supervisor separate, nothing to see here.

Mikey's flimsy fantasia dissolves, instantly hardening back into the rock of raw reality. The scenery is restored to exactly what it was before this brief idyllic intermezzo.

Through some backwards legerdemain, the rest of the guards materialize.

Supervisor divides them into teams of two and gives out the day's work assignments.

They all hold hands in a circle, bow heads, and mumble-pray that they survive the shift unharmed.

The duos disperse to their respective posts, except Mikey, who follows the Supervisor off, memorizing the racy undulation of her scrumptious rump for inspiration during Pleasure Breaks.

Georgie, today Mikey's teammate, takes his place in front of the closed Curtain, the centerpiece of the Property.

Mikey joins him.

They survey the area for suspicious individuals or activity, inspect the Fourth Wall for holes, and park themselves each at the opposite side of the proscenium arch, poised to pounce at the puniest hint of peril. Every moment's fraught with threat.

Their minds wander, obsess about what's behind the

Curtain. All they've been told is no one's allowed to come near it, let alone touch it.

But nothing happens, which in itself is suspicious, given the strategic importance of their post.

Georgie is in charge of paperwork and logs it.

The Log is a record of threats perceived or actually thwarted, which at the end of the shift are tallied and measured against their quota, determining their emolument.

Mikey and Georgie are not only colleagues, but also best friends. They get along so well, they could win the Nobel Prize for Chemistry.

Despite strict rules of conduct on post, they always find ingenious and subtle ways to have fun and horse around.

Both are former thespians, bona fide triple-threats, actor-singer-dancers, but as talking on post is an absolute no-no, dance is, by default, their only available outlet.

During longish lulls in activity, before tedium sets in and robs them of élan, to kill time before it kills them, they've been channeling their pent-up creativity into staging a cute little dance number, a playful *pas de deux*, which epitomizes their profound friendship.

Usually, after reviewing the last eight counts from the

previous secret practice, they pick up where they left off and add a few more moves.

One of them, this time it's Mikey, proposes a short sequence of steps, which the other one quickly learns. They then repeat the new section together over and over until they're happy.

They've been working on the dance every chance they get, risking their jobs, hoping in the end to enter the finished product into one of the many talent contests on TV, win, and get back to living their dream.

But progress is slow; something always interrupts their surreptitious rehearsals.

A shadow flies over them, accompanied by a gust of fragrant wind.

They look up to identify its source.

Nothing there. Ominous.

When they look down, the shadow has transmuted into an individual.

Mikey and Georgie feel self-conscious, probably the worst emotion on stage, and get together for safety in numbers, overcome with what can only be described as stage fright, except it's totally different.

For security guards, they are a skittish pair, but what

else can be expected from erstwhile entertainers, whose careers were built on fears, phobias, and insecurities?

The individual before them is unremarkable, non-threatening.

He reminds Mikey of his Grandmother, bless her immortal, immoral soul.

But guards are trained not to be fooled by appearances; the more innocuous a suspect appears, the more potentially dangerous he is. They brace themselves.

This seemingly harmless male nonchalantly walks along the Fourth Wall, posing no perceivable threat whatsoever, his true intentions illegible.

Mikey and Georgie don't know what to do and squirm in consternation. There are gaping holes in the logic of this situation. They're unqualified to deal with the ineffable.

Mikey notices something peculiar about him. On his head, there are two nubs where horns used to be and have been sawed off.

They realize that he is none other than his Eminence, the Prince of Darkness, the Devil himself.

He's not as ostentatious as his legend, but extra too ordinary, like he works in an office, a junior accountant in a tax prep firm. Either the Devil is the opposite of who they thought he was, completely misunderstood, or he's being played by a bad actor who hasn't done his research. Or, the scariest alternative, the Devil can assume the shape of our worst fears.

They know they should do something, at least out of respect for the Devil's past achievements, but wait for him to make the first move. Security guards, like actors, are most powerless against inaction.

No doubt the Devil knows this, and continues to mind his own business, not hurting anyone, looking around aimlessly like a common breed of dumb tourist.

What does it say about their profession as security guards that the Devil himself, supposedly the baddest of the bad guys, presents no danger? What is their purpose, their motivation? What are they doing here?

Mikey's experiencing severe Actor's Block, a common affliction in the performing arts community, gateway into alcoholism, drug abuse, chronic adultery, and other types of cancer.

Staring at the dull Devil, they feel useless. Their job makes no sense. The metaphorical floor beneath them opens, and they vertigo, in unison, into an existential crisis, the only real Hell, probably the Devil's plan all along.

But Mikey isn't one to wallow in negative emotions too long and decides to apprehend the celebrity suspect. Act first, ask questions later, a standard security practice.

As per protocol, they circumnavigate the Devil to neutralize his threat potential. But their over-rehearsed maneuver has zero effect. The Devil couldn't be more neutral already, showing no interest in the Property at all. Either he doesn't know its value, or knows something they don't, that it has no value.

They are stumped, wishing someone smart were here to tell them what to do.

A *corps de ballet* of female Questions and male Doubts cavort across the stage.

Mikey waits for inspiration.

It doesn't come.

He changes location; maybe it flows better elsewhere.

Inspiration does come, but in the form of a translucent butterfly.

Mikey has a phobia of butterflies, which is strange, because he loves butter.

It chases him around.

Georgie, sensing his friend's distress, shoos the insolent insect away.

They'll have to do without inspiration. It's overrated anyway.

Finally the Devil turns to study the Curtain.

Mikey and Georgie start moving toward him stealthily so as not to spook him.

But as they approach, the Devil swivels, and glides between them.

They look stupid.

He gets too close to the precious Curtain, putting it in jeopardy.

Mikey and Georgie, now with probable cause, go to apprehend him again.

But before they reach him, the Devil explodes, and poof, disappears in a cloud of orange smoke that smells like cheddar cheese.

When the smoke clears and they finish coughing, Georgie discovers some suspicious substance on the floor.

They inspect it visually.

Orange powder with bits of solid matter.

Mikey touches it and sucks his finger.

Georgie thinks that's a bad idea but is too curious to stop his friend.

Mikey concludes it's Cheetos, the most disarming

comestible on the market, practically a weaponized snack, a potent paralytic agent, capable of reducing everyone in its presence into a simple eating machine.

They deliberate. It's a biohazard.

While Mikey wages war on his urge to lick the floor, Georgie talks into his sleeve, requests cleanup, and logs the incident.

Mikey conquers his inner glutton and joins Georgie.

They secure the perimeter around the Cheetos and wait for the Janitor.

He skates in with a cordless vacuum cleaner.

It tries to eat Mikey's shoes.

Mikey feels disrespected, accuses the Janitor of anti-Semitism, and psychs himself up for an altercation.

The Janitor, too cowardly to deal with consequences of his ostensibly bigoted behavior, steers the vacuum cleaner away, and skates off with a satisfied smile, leaving Mikey holding an armful of burning grudge.

Georgie logs it as Mikey struggles to regain composure.

Eventually they resume their normal routine.

The monotony is broken when Big Boss brings by the Client who's hired the Agency to guard the Property.

They're escorting what looks like a delegation of

nouveau riche Russo-Chinese Oligarchs on a world-tour shopping spree.

All stop in front of the Curtain.

Mikey and Georgie are nervous and act busier than they need to be.

Big Boss behaves in an embarrassingly obsequious manner. At one point he takes the Client's hand and bites it, all in good fun, to release the palpable tension in the air. It's his way of establishing intimacy and trust.

The Client takes it in stride, no doubt having encountered much worse in the entertainment business.

Meanwhile, the supposed Oligarchs leap about in front of the Curtain, acting shifty.

It's hard to corral them within Mikey's and Georgie's fields of vision, a classic Russo-Chinese ruse to disorient their opponent. Mikey and Georgie feel like sheep dogs punished to guard a herd of arrogant goats.

Oligarchs start taking flash photos, a red flag.

Mikey reprimands them with a stiff index finger.

They look at the Client for permission.

He nods, it's ok.

Mikey and Georgie turn to Big Boss for backup.

He shrugs and shows them his hands, like they're tied.

The delegation laughs.

Mikey and Georgie feel undermined, ridiculed, resentful.

To rub it in, the obnoxious Oligarchs request a group photo in front of the Curtain, which they're planning to buy along with the rest of the world. They arrange themselves around the Client.

Mikey and Georgie, disgusted, step out of frame.

But the Russo-Chinese have the audacity to insist they get in the shot.

Reluctantly, Mikey and Georgie pose with them. Fake cheese.

Big Boss takes the picture, and they leap off. A portentous cloud of suspicion lingers after them.

Mikey and Georgie are mad and take it out on each other. Why did no one inform them about this? It could have been an international scandal.

Just for that, Georgie diligently logs each member of the delegation as a separate incident, embellishing salient points for dramatic impact. This entry alone will ensure that they meet their quota for the day, making the rest of the shift a frivolous formality.

Mikey slows down his racing heart and lowers his blood pressure.

He reads over Georgie's shoulder.

Impeccable penmanship. Georgie's notation system is intimidating, each incident broken down into sub-incidents, which are parsed even further. He's able to perceive potential for danger in every micro-gesture and express it in pithy poetic prose of unparalleled precision.

Mikey would eat anything to have Georgie's writing talent.

But all of a sudden Georgie is depressed. He gets down on himself too easily, the curse of true genius; it never knows its own worth.

Mikey's concerned, tries to help.

Georgie won't let him, wants to be left alone.

Mikey's feelings are hurt.

But he's been swallowing so much pride already, what's another mouthful? He invades Georgie's personal space.

Georgie continues to ignore him, the worst you can do to Mikey, the consummate actor, deny him attention, the thing he craves above all, his entire *raison d'etre*.

He interrogates Georgie, playing good cop and bad cop respectively.

Georgie avoids eye-contact.

Mikey's tenacious, aggressively friendly.

But this leads nowhere good. Georgie leaves him no choice but to assault him physically.

They tussle.

Mikey beats him.

They almost crash through the Curtain.

He tortures his friend until he agrees to tell him what he wants to hear.

Georgie confesses he's in love, which by itself wouldn't be the worst, but of all the eligible individuals he could be in love with, he's in love with the one individual Mikey's in love with, their Supervisor.

Impossible, inconceivable, an anathema, Mikey screams in his head. Bile bubbles up into his throat. This is a slap in the face, basically an assault on the sacred institution of friendship.

He wants to beat him more, but tears himself away.

He paces his invisible cage, rides the rollercoaster of rage, his blood boiling, scalding his insides, singeing his reason.

He could seriously kill Georgie, but he can't imagine life without him.

Further interrogation reveals that Georgie hasn't told her yet, so not all is lost, although he plans to declare his love to her next time they're alone.

It's Mikey's turn to act depressed.

Georgie interrogates him.

Mikey can't even, cannot look at him, avoids eye-contact.

Georgie invades his personal space. And so forth. They repeat verbatim their earlier choreography, except switch parts.

Instead of telling Georgie that he was first and Supervisor rightly belongs to him, and asking him to stay away from her, Mikey tries to convince his BFF that getting romantically involved with her is a terrible terrible idea, overdramatizing all the horrific consequences, using arguments that he himself would best heed, like that she is married, and to the Big Boss, nonetheless, who, if he finds out, will fire Georgie.

But Georgie doesn't care; his love for her is too strong and apparently indestructible.

Mikey panics. He is forced to make up awful lies about the woman he loves more than anything, with the exception of Georgie; they occupy the same space in his heart. He resents that it may come to having to choose between them. He needs them both, and in their right roles, the ones he cast them in.

He proceeds to assassinate her character, criticizes her appearance, pointing out all her superficial flaws, attempting to persuade Georgie the bitch ain't even worth it, almost, in the moment, dangerously close to believing it himself.

It makes no difference to Georgie.

Mikey's despondent. His universe shrinks to the size of the little muscle inside his chest, a hundred grams of frantic flesh.

Georgie and Mikey, a galaxy of two sore hearts orbiting each other.

A fresh challenge brings them back to Earth.

A hoary old woman breaches the perimeter of the invisible red zone. She smells delicious, but looks unpalatable, appears intoxicated, and careens around, putting the Property in jeopardy.

The guards of this Agency are drilled never to underestimate the elderly, who have little to lose, plenty to prove, and are reckless with their short leftover lives, widowed grannies especially, looking for the last fuck you to the immutably male-dominated world. With them diplomacy is not an option. Mikey knows this from personal experience, his dead Grandmother.

He and Georgie position themselves between her and the Curtain, willing to waste their lives defending it.

She charges them like a crazy cow.

They tackle her, and take all their frustrations out on her, personal and professional.

She thrashes around like a fish on land with more strength than a woman her size and age should scientifically have.

The threesome rolls around on the floor in a fast forward cartoon ball of disembodied body parts, grunting like pork, her dentures snapping at the air like a territorial turtle.

Mikey almost loses a finger.

It takes their combined maximum muscle to immobilize her.

Georgie realizes she is actually their Supervisor in disguise.

Mikey, mentally more sluggish, also soon figures out who she is.

The scene freezes in a still frame.

Their addled brains scramble to add up all the new info. This is only a drill, they conclude, a routine test of their alertness. Suddenly everything makes perfect sense, including their boners.

But this is also an opportunity. They play dumber than they are, and resume grinding on her, groping taboo regions of her camouflaged body.

Before the situation blooms into a full-blown *ménage a trois*, Supervisor disentangles herself from the octopus of their lusty limbs.

Mikey and Georgie, from inertia, continue dry-humping each other. Flesh is flesh; if you cross and squint your eyes, it's all the same.

She takes off her grotesque mask and garment and watches them with bemusement.

They stop just short of orgasm, get up, brush and straighten out uniforms. Their erections linger a while longer.

Georgie apologizes for both of them.

Mikey doesn't believe they did anything wrong, but assures her it won't happen again, though he hopes it will.

She congratulates them on passing the test, minus minor mistakes, but nobody's perfect.

They puff up with pride. Her compliments renew their faith in the job and reset their sense of purpose.

Supervisor consults her assignments roster, checks her watch, and reminds Mikey it's time for his scheduled Pleasure Break. She'll cover for him until he returns.

Normally this would be a cause for a yippee and a celebratory jumping jack, there's nothing Mikey looks forward to more than Pleasure Breaks, but knowing what he knows about Georgie's designs on her heart, he turns it down. Mikey's good, fresh as new, a frisky biscuit.

But she insists. Pleasure Breaks are mandatory, an indispensable form of emotional hygiene.

Mikey offers to forfeit his break to Georgie, who is younger, and therefore has a larger libido to relieve, a bigger reservoir of seminal fluid buildup, which if he doesn't empty, he's gambling with prostate cancer.

She admonishes him that it's against regulations to swap Pleasure Breaks.

The last thing Mikey wants is to upset her, give her ammo to be unfaithful, and grudgingly shuffles off, pouting like a little bitch, grumbling under his breath.

Needless to say, Mikey's Pleasure Break is a monumental waste of time, a damn disaster. As usual, he locks himself in his favorite toilet stall, on whose walls, as autoerotic pabulum, he normally projects mental pornographic movies starring a handsome version of him and the Supervisor.

But in his current upset state, all he can visualize is Georgie and her talking, laughing, touching, flirting, all sans sound, like a silent movie, and since he can't decipher what they're saying, he imagines the worst.

Still, out of habit, he makes a withdrawal of a few recycled images deposited in his spank-bank, spits on his hand, and tries to whisk up a workable boner.

But it only leads to a dry dead end. Frustrating.

Mikey believes he's losing everything he has, both his best friend and his virtual lover, and feels forsaken.

This toilet, which at least thrice daily is his treat, a retreat from troubles, a synagogue of serenity, is now some Satanic temple of torture.

It fills with shady characters. They rip the door off Mikey's stall, drag him outside, pants and undies around his ankles, and prance around him.

They're his Personal Demons. Most of them he hasn't seen in years, thought he'd gotten over them for good, and others have brought plus ones, total strangers.

They came to party, evidently, pick him up, and pass

him around like a flaccid blowup doll, each doing a dumb duet with his helpless frame.

Things could be worse, Mikey consoles himself, and immediately is proven right.

The smallest Demon, a child or a midget, hard to tell, punches him in the nuts.

Mikey groans and drapes himself over the toilet bowl, which now serves as a sacrificial altar, his exposed butt cheeks invitingly in the air.

Four full-grown Demons hold him down while the little one approaches from behind, his penis disproportionately large.

Mikey has the wherewithal to partially pull his dirty drawers over his anus, obstructing easy entry.

But it only peeves them off. He becomes the centerpiece of a gargantuan gangbang. They sodomize him unconscious.

When he wakes up, crumpled on the floor of the flooded stall, every orifice in his body sore, he's alone.

He washes his hands and face and gargles Demon semen out of his mouth. In the mirror, he fixes his uniform, hair, and makeup, glues himself back together as best he can. Good to go again, only slightly more broken, but that's normal life as Mikey understands it, a nonstop incremental process of degradation.

He returns to post, his recent trauma hidden under a triple layer of concealer, everything hunky-dory, total professionalism.

The entire population of his emotional world—Georgie, Supervisor, and Big Boss—is impatiently waiting for him.

Big Boss is anxious, on the verge of tears.

Supervisor's hands are all over him.

Mikey doesn't need to see that.

Georgie's jealous too.

Mikey would feel bad for him if he wasn't already feeling bad for himself.

Apparently the Client's complaining that the Agency's charging too exorbitant a fee, but nothing's happening; he's not getting his money's worth.

Perhaps he's missing the point? Aren't they here precisely so that nothing happens? The Agency measures their success by how little they do. Security is the ultimate anti-accomplishment business.

But the Client was expecting more action, and accuses the Agency of false advertising, even questioning the authenticity of the rave reviews of their past work excerpted in their promo brochure, which boast that they are the most entertaining security outfit the New Ruble can buy, whereas in actuality, judging by their performance here so far, they are the most boring.

Oh no he didn't, use the B-word, the absolute worst insult to any performing artist, retired or active.

But it's his money. The Client has the sacrosanct right to get exactly what he believes he's paying for. If entertainment's what he wants, then entertainment is what he shall get. Otherwise he threatens to hire a replacement company.

Mikey, Georgie, and Supervisor rally around Big Boss, and earnestly pay attention to his directions, confident they can act their way out of any predicament.

They initiate Code E, pure exhibition mode, and prepare to perform an aestheticized dramatization of an actual attack they once thwarted, the one for which they're famous and their good reputation is based on.

Half the ensemble, Georgie among them, goes off to change into Bad Guy costumes that the Agency stole from the very Bad Guys they fought that legendary day, a competing security firm intent on sabotaging their then gig.

Mikey will play a Good Guy, again. The management

doesn't trust him yet to portray a more complex evil character, which he's bitter about.

Supervisor leads her delicate husband away.

Mikey can't watch.

It's been a while since they did this particular routine, so each guard quickly reviews the basic staging and marks through the choreography. The place is a flurry of individual pre-show rituals.

Mikey skims over the highlighted sections of his Stanislavsky Pocket Bible, more from superstition than necessity, as he has the whole book memorized, brushes up on his backstory, does a painful sense memory exercise, and gets positively pumped.

Everyone takes a quiet me-moment to get in character.

Alarums! The Curtain is attacked by a chorus of pretend Bad Guys.

Mikey defends it valiantly.

His reinforcements arrive, late, having missed their cue, but better than never.

Quote unquote Bad Guys also multiply, evening out the numbers on both sides.

They're so well costumed that Mikey can't tell it's really his colleagues, or which one of them is Georgie. The consummate Method actor, he's getting progressively deeper into his character and losing the ability to distinguish reality from fiction.

The fight is a fine fandango of Oriental martial arts, East-Euro circus acrobatics, pretentious West-Euro modernist dance, good ol' 'merican fake wrestlin', ye olde bare-knuckle fisticuffs, and elements of male baboons fighting over females and territory the Agency copied from a National Geographic TV documentary. They are doing faux flips, somersaults, cartwheels, and air karate chops accompanied by racist onomatopoeias, and other unmotivated moves.

Some falls look painful, but add the right amount of naturalism to deliver the desired emotional punch. Stupid audiences love stupid actors really hurting one another.

Both blood types, fake and real, are drawn.

The wounded are attended to by two ex-actors sharing one nurse costume, for budgetary reasons.

In the absence of genuine feeling and deep character work, there's a lot of overacting.

But only two or three times is the Curtain in realistic danger due to performer error.

It's unclear who's losing. Both sides are equally inept.

The Client is watching the show from a safe distance, impersonating an ignorant critic, not that there is any other kind.

Big Boss and Supervisor are shamelessly fawning around him, ardently praying for approval. This is a lucrative contract they can't afford to lose. The future of the Agency hinges on it.

But the guards are so egregiously out of shape that soon they tire physically and start hurting one another's feelings, hurling cheap insults at the opponent, mostly regarding appearance, with an occasional half-hearted pushing and effeminate slapping. The production slows down to a quarter tempo, taking on a mid-week matinee malaise.

Then, pandemonium erupts.

An embarrassment of fugitive, disoriented pandas sprints across the stage before anyone can figure out what the fuck.

Mikey notices his coworkers are fighting as if their own, not their characters', lives depended on it. Where did this sudden surge of urgency come from? This is not the choreography they spent months perfecting. All vestiges of technique and proper form fly out the proverbial window. If what they were doing before had little artistic merit, what they're doing now has none. This is sheer realism, no stylization, the antithesis of the Agency's signature style.

Mikey also finds himself involved in a true brawl. He's kicked in the head. No one from his Agency can kick that high. He's kicked again, from the other side. Twinkling stars above. He swats them away.

There appears to be a surplus of Bad Guys. Or he's seeing in duplicate, a symptom of concussion. The Good Guys are outnumbered two to one.

He recognizes the new faces. They're the same individuals who several scenes ago came through as the delegation of Russo-Chinese Oligarchs. He knew something was up with them, but no one listens to a lowly guard.

In actuality, they're the members of the Band of Ballet Bandits, formerly known as Ballet Russe, a rival security company, their main competitor, the very one that narrowly lost the battle being reenacted, and whose costumes half of Mikey's colleagues are presently wearing. The Bandits are back, better and badder, their bodies fresh and fit, lean and mean, with vengeance in their eyes.

They leap about *en pointe* like ethereal fairies, enthralling the guards with grace.

These ex-ballerinas and ballerinoes have reconfigured

their obsolete medium into a martial art. They're using their lanky limbs as weapons, maiming their enemy with piquant pirouettes and risqué arabesques. Who knew toe shoes were perfect for knocking out teeth?

But the Ballet Bandits, surprisingly, aren't interested in the Curtain at all. It seems they just want their clothing back, because they proceed to undress their identically-clad counterparts, who lack the stamina to resist.

Then, in retaliation for embarrassing them before, they even strip the rest of the guards of their uniforms and undergarments.

Mikey too loses all his clothes.

It doesn't stop him. This is his chance to prove his worth. He accesses emergency reserves of energy deep within, and turns into a tornado of teeth and fingernails, attacking every tutu and leotard indiscriminately. Better safe than sorry.

Bad Guys begin retreating, their retrieved costumes and pilfered uniforms plus soiled skivvies stuffed in their spandex.

The guards are slithering around in front of the Curtain *au naturel* like a lounge of delirious, paraplegic lizards.

The Bandits forget one of their own,

uncharacteristically undignified, pathetically whimpering and rocking on the ground, face hidden in his hands.

Maybe the Agency can keep him as a POW, use him for negotiating the return of their uniforms, or at least the underwear, depending on how much he's worth to them.

Mikey pounces on the ballerino like a famished puma, direct for the man's groin, his foamy maw missing his manhood by mere millimeters, and bites down on the inside of his right thigh, the tenderest, arguably the most flavorful part of human physiognomy. The more the hostage bandit writhes and wiggles, struggles to wriggle out, the harder Mikey sinks his teeth into his flesh, breaking skin, severing the femoral artery. A load of hot blood spurts inside his mouth, hitting the back of his throat.

Luckily, Mikey has no gag reflex, rips out a hunk of lean meat, and skulks away to chew in peace.

A burly pair of Ballet Bandits returns, stops in disgust and or horror. But instead of dragging off their injured mate, they only remove his garb and flee without him.

The place looks like one of those typical Oklahoma nudist colonies after a tornado.

The crippled guard corps crawl away to lick their wounds and bitch in the Green Room.

Mikey's alone with the naked man he's mauled.

To his dismay, he realizes it's Georgie. He's bleeding out. Mikey's bite, unless promptly treated, could be lethal.

How convenient to mortally wound, or near emasculate, his prime romantic rival.

But he pleads not guilty; it wasn't premeditated, an honest mistake. Mikey swears on his Grandmother's untended, unattended grave.

He tries to plug the fatal hole in Georgie's thigh with a finger.

Georgie convulses in agony.

Now that it's safe, Supervisor and Big Boss arrive. They blame Mikey for everything. It's not hard to make him feel bad; he was born with congenital guilt.

Big Boss famously hates the sight of blood and looks askance at the hyperventilating Georgie.

Georgie's fighting for every breath; each could be his last.

Supervisor examines him.

Georgie faints.

She tries to resuscitate him.

Big Boss, to look busy, checks Mikey for injuries, first visually, then manually, his hands roaming randomly over his flabbergasted body, losing himself in the subtext of the task, until his wife rouses him.

She urges they take Georgie to the hospital ASAP.

Big Boss thinks it would be a waste of effort; he's too far gone.

She insists then on taking him there herself.

He mocks her, calling hospitals glorified slaughterhouses, supermarkets for human organs, and they should just let Georgie bleed out in piece and die with dignity.

But she is adamant.

They step aside for a quickie marital tiff.

Mikey gets a private moment with Georgie. He administers First Aid, shaking him and yelling, hang in there buddy, breathe, don't quit me now.

It works. Georgie opens his eyes.

Mikey re-apologizes, so profusely it borders on disingenuous. He offers to hurt himself if it would make his friend feel better, and gnaws on his forearm.

Georgie stops him, forgives him.

Mikey's moved to tears and exaggerates wiping his eyes so Georgie can see the effect his magnanimity has on him.

Georgie reaches out his hand, holding the Log. He

wants Mikey to have a keepsake of him in case he doesn't make it.

Nonsense, of course he'll make it, his injury is not that serious, Mikey lies. But he'll happily safeguard the little notebook until his recovery. He takes it, solemnly presses it against his heart, and promises that on the off-chance Georgie doesn't indeed make it, he'll forever treasure the precious gift.

Georgie loses consciousness again.

The quarreling couple reenters.

Big Boss storms off in a huff like a disgraced diva.

Supervisor knows what buttons to push.

She pushes Mikey aside like he's furniture, and picks up Georgie.

In spite of himself, Mikey is impressed and falls in love with her all over again. There is nothing hotter than a female holding in her arms a male that's twice her size.

She carries Georgie's nearly lifeless body away to the hospital.

On his hands and knees in a pool of his best friend's blood, Mikey's feeling sorry for himself.

Someone skates in and stops over him.

Mikey lifts his eyes.

It's his archenemy, the Janitor, lazily leaning on the butt of a mop handle, looking down at Mikey condescendingly. He smirks and shakes his head, like he knew all along this is exactly how Mikey'd end up, shattered into million little puzzle pieces that would never fit back together.

Mikey gathers the leftovers of his physical resources and starts getting up. But he's too weak, and plops back down into the juice.

Janitor sniggers and proceeds to mop the floor, mostly just pushing the viscous liquid around, smearing it everywhere like he's painting some giant abstract expressionist mess.

Mikey, boiling over with impotent rage, drags himself away before he's further humiliated, vowing to some day soon exact revenge.

He takes the rest of the day off.

At home, to get his mind off the earlier tragedy, he picks up his well-worn copy of beloved Stanislavsky, a guaranteed source of joy and inspiration, and starts reading from the beginning for the umpteenth time.

But something's wonky with his vision. The words keep rearranging themselves on the page, frantically bumping into one another like a colony of horny sperm under a microscope.

His body's tired, but his mind is restless, raring to race.

He isn't hungry, but goes to eat anyway; it's something to do. Inside the fridge it's warmer than a sauna and smells like a third-world morgue. All his meat's gone bad.

Never mind, his cupboards are stocked with emergency jerky, and he improvises a kind of jerky taco, the perfect assuasive snack.

But it too tastes tainted.

He lays out his masturbation paraphernalia. He's uninspired, but goes for it regardless. It feels like self-rape and he gives up after several lackluster strokes. He fears he'll never feel pleasure again.

He is distrait, gets depressed, and trudges around the apartment heavy-footed.

Guilt has eaten a hole in his conscience. Mikey sees Georgie's face superimposed everywhere.

He sits down to write him a letter, confess everything, and ask him nicely to leave Supervisor alone.

He has Writer's Block and ends up stabbing the stationary to death with his pen.

Uninvited guests arrive. About a dozen of his Personal

Demons, the All-Star team, turn his humble home into their den.

Their most recent rendezvous didn't work out so well for Mikey, and given the trend that every time they get together, the Demons take it up a notch, he doesn't expect this one to go any better.

But all he can do is be a passive spectator to their fiendish shenanigans.

One of them is mock-declaiming the same passage of Stanislavsky Mikey couldn't read earlier, staining the pages with sticky barbecue-sauce fingers.

Is really nothing sacred to them?

Maybe coffee would perk him up, give him strength to stand up to them. But they are molesting his coffee machine, making it fart and burp, so much so that he can't see himself ever using it again.

They eat all his meat. It doesn't matter that it's green; common parasites don't affect common Demons.

Mikey doesn't interfere.

Only when they get into his protein powder and make a mess does he get involved and snatches the container away.

They don't appreciate that.

He gets in bed, exhausted, hoping to sleep off this odious visitation.

The aggravated ghouls jump in with him.

But something's stirring in the sheets.

Everyone freezes.

It's the Devil. He comes out and cozies up to Mikey, sleepy-eyed, yawning.

Demons hiss and scurry.

Mikey's scared, cowers under the covers.

But the Devil puts him at ease again with his uncanny resemblance to his Grandmother.

He endeavors to talk Mikey out of feeling guilty for hurting Georgie, he was just doing his job, and works on allaying Mikey's negative self-image, reminding him of all the good he's done, the animals and individuals he's helped, his Grandmother, for instance, when she was dying, and so forth, and he shouldn't care what anybody thinks of him, just be himself.

Mikey's unconvinced.

The Devil uses examples from his own scandalous past to illustrate that Mikey's not, comparatively, a bad person; he is proud of Mikey, and Mikey should be proud of himself.

And so he is.

But being suspicious by nature and profession, he also wonders what's in it for the Devil. Is this the classic bait and switch, first session's free, and then, when you're hooked, you have to pay? Mikey could easily get addicted to feeling this great.

But his soul is not for sale.

The Devil, however, doesn't seem to be shopping, either. It never comes up.

Mikey lays his suspicions aside. It doesn't matter, ultimately. Thanks to the Devil, he feels better than ever, and that's all that counts.

Finally, the Devil takes Mikey's hand and squeezes.

Is it over? Mikey wants to hug him, but by the time he gets up the courage, as usual, it's too late.

After fluffing Mikey's pillow, the Devil throws that cheesy orange powder in the air, and disappears back under the sheets.

Even though Mikey's missing the Devil already, an involuntary smile plays upon his lips. For the first time he feels fantastic in his own skin, not too tight and not too loose, un-conflicted, and stays as still as possible, lest if he moves, he scares the sensation away.

But nothing good, by definition, lasts forever. That's show business.

Soon the bellicose hobgoblins, his Personal Demons, reinvade his home and assault him.

Emboldened by the fact the Devil's in his corner, Mikey frees himself from their grabby paws and absquatulates to the bathroom, locking the door.

He sits on the toilet and sighs, thinks about Supervisor. Where is she? What is she doing? Did she stay with Georgie in the hospital or just drop him off? Should Mikey be at the hospital?

Demons start banging on the door, twisting the knob.

Mikey remembers Georgie's Log, takes it out, reads a random page. It's a masterpiece, practically a manifesto on style and substance, crystalline simplicity incarnate, not a syllable of verbose fat, zero tortured illiterate alliterations, torturous verbal contortions, no silly similes and mangled metaphors, braggadocious verbiage that wannabe word-smiths self-indulge in to compensate for the banality of their content.

But it's too soon, the tragedy too fresh. Reading the Log only exacerbates Mikey's anguish.

He hides it behind the toilet so that no one can find it.

Demons have meanwhile begun breaking down the door.

Mikey has to get out of here, and pronto, expeditiously.

In a dirty laundry hamper he finds his workout clothes. They're still damp and smell spicy from the last time he exercised. He puts them on anyway.

When he's dressed, he throws open the door.

The Demons come crashing in and pile on top of each other.

He locks them inside, and hurries outside.

The street is empty and quiet.

Mikey starts running, first lightly, for warm-up, then harder. He's out of shape, but it's good to punish the body, short-circuiting the mind so it has to power down and recuperate. All Mikey hears is his arrhythmic breath.

But soon enough, behind him, there's a cacophony of wheezing, huffing, puffing, and syncopated footsteps, more like hoof-steps.

When he looks back, there they are, his Personal Demons, stampeding after him, their eyes burning red with rage.

In the past, he's always been able to outrun them. If he knows one thing about his Demons, it's that they are lazy and allergic to sweat. But they're keeping up with him. Shows how much he knows.

You don't know anything if you don't know your own demons.

Mikey speeds up.

So do they, gaining on him, getting close, their animus toward him at an all-time high. They seem extra motivated to catch him, even more than he is to escape.

Two of the truculent trolls are already grabbing at his backside. He knows where this is going.

Truth is, he's only a little less lazy than they are, and thinks about giving up, letting them have their way with him. How bad can it really be? They couldn't possibly hurt him more than he's already hurting himself.

But ahead, on the next block, he spots a Church, the one place, he assumes, no self-respecting demon would deign enter.

Mikey engages his afterburners and sprints towards it, leaving his pursuers cursing in the dust.

He goes in. By the entrance, he catches his breath and drinks a handful of holy water, both from thirst and for good luck.

He feels self-conscious in his soggy tank top and jogging

short shorts, underdressed for Church, and hides behind a column, from where he surveys the place.

The nave of the Church is a hive of activity. All the pews have been moved to the sides and arranged like theater-in-the-round, Mikey's least favorite configuration.

A rapt audience is watching a ballet recital accompanied on an organ from above.

Mikey too becomes engrossed.

The ballet seems familiar, like he's seen it before, perhaps a classic everyone's supposed to know, a staple of any reputable ballet company.

He recognizes the dancers. It's the Band of Ballet Bandits. Disbelief distorts his vision.

He shakes his head back into focus, a kind of double-take, the move he was famous for throughout his acting career. He's inadvertently walked into the enemy nest.

It dawns on him he's witnessing a reenactment of the latest battle between the Bandits and Mikey's Agency, half the dancers wearing stolen uniforms, playing crude caricatures of the guards, a silly farce.

One of the ballerinas is portraying Mikey, which would normally be flattering, no one's ever considered him interesting enough to turn him into a fictional character, but she's doing a terrible job. This is not at all how he perceives himself, as an obese effeminate buffoon, but rather as a tragic hero. He fights the urge to go on stage and show her how it's done.

Then, in the corner among other refuse, Mikey spots a pile of his Agency's uniforms, those not being used in the show, tossed there haphazardly, a flagrant display of disrespect, a provocation almost. His blood pressure climbs to a nearly lethal level.

This is his chance to redeem himself. He's going to steal the uniforms back. He tiptoes towards them and picks them up. But while clumsily arranging them in his arms, he knocks over a cruciform tired Jesus leaning on the wall. It makes a loud noise that echoes through the Church.

The beefy ballerina who is playing Mikey stops twirling like a drunk tornado, pivots her head towards the clangor, points at Mikey, and yells something in an ugly foreign language, Russian or Chinese, or a hybrid of the two, Russianese.

The room turns to him. The organ grinds to a hostile silence. Everyone glares.

Mikey freezes, his face a gargoyled rictus, and holds his breath, trying to pass for a statue of a saint, which is hard in his tank and booty shorts. He starts to shake from lack of oxygen, exhales a robust gust of stale air, and coughs.

The congregation of ungentle gentiles starts creeping toward him.

He better leave. But outside, he remembers, his Personal Demons are still most likely waiting for him.

Panic-stricken, he looks around for a hole to hide in. There's nothing.

He has only two options, either be gang-raped by Demons or by former ballerinas. He deliberates which is worse. At least he knows his Demons' venereal preferences and is inured to their abuse, but who knows to what kinky ordeals the wily Russianese might subject his body and soul?

He stops pontificating and skedaddles, resigned to whatever fate, the terrifying tap tap of toe shoes after him.

His Personal Demons, shocker, are loitering out front, vandalizing Church property.

But to Mikey's amazement, they don't notice him.

He almost manages to sneak past them, when the Band of Ballet Bandits and their devout posse emerge from their luxurious lair and screech to a halt, vexed at the sight of the sizeable assembly.

Demons regroup and refocus.

Mikey's surrounded, bummer, caught between two gangs, a tasty treat in the middle that everyone's drooling over.

Bandits and Demons stare at each other hatefully, both laying claim to Mikey as their rightful prize.

It's been a while since he felt so desired, like never, and the dumb half of him basks even in this negative attention.

Demons insist they own Mikey and only they get to victimize him.

Bandits counter that he's trespassed on their territory and stolen costumes, the evidence still in his arms.

Mikey protests the uniforms belong to the Agency he works for.

Nobody's listening to anybody; the argument's foredoomed.

Both sides move in on Mikey, equally determined to make him their bitch.

Instinctively, to free his hands so he can defend at least his combover hairdo, Mikey throws the uniforms in the air.

Upon descent, they land on his assailants' heads, temporarily blinding them.

He uses this welcome happenstance to crawl out of the melee.

Bandits and Demons recover their sight and pummel each other in a messy mosh pit.

Lucky Mikey escapes unscathed.

They eventually realize that the object of their rage has gotten away, feel dumb, agree to work together, look for the fugitive, locate him in the distance, and chase after him.

Mikey does the worst thing an individual in his circumstance can do: he looks back over his shoulder. It's practically a sign of capitulation and slows him down considerably.

The multi-headed but single-minded dragon's about to devour him.

His bad knee is screaming, his lungs are in flames, his throat's clogged with phlegm, and he wants to quit.

But he can't. An obsessive-compulsive notion has settled in his brain that if he stops running, or even slows down, Georgie will die for sure. Mikey's extremely superstitious, and keeps racing for his best friend's life across multiple thresholds of pain.

For motivation, he pictures Georgie in the Intensive Care Unit attached to hoses, cables, and assorted life-saving and monitoring gadgetry, his injured leg bandaged too tight, turned purple and swollen twice its normal size.

This is when Mikey regrets his life choices, like attending the acting academy instead of medical school.

But then, he has an epiphany. It would be a damn shame not to take advantage of Georgie's absence. Otherwise his death, if it does occur, will be for nothing. Mikey could never forgive himself.

His new genius idea is to confess to Big Boss that he's in love with his wife. She's intimated, indirectly, that her husband is the only obstacle standing in the way of their amour. Then, respectfully, man to man, he'll ask for Big Boss's permission, even a blessing, to take the affair to the next level and officially consummate it, while reassuring him that in no way is he interested in breaking up their marriage, the holiest of unions, as long as there's some wiggle room in it for him.

Big Boss is an open-minded, artsy individual, an ex-theater director, a latter-day liberal, so he's bound to understand.

This would also preempt Supervisor's romantic involvement with Georgie. What Mikey would be doing, essentially, he believes, is saving his BFF from himself, protecting him from inevitable heartbreak.

It's a win win for everyone. Mikey's smart.

Big Boss's and Supervisor's apartment building, conveniently, just happens to be in the area, right around the corner.

Mikey makes a sudden sharp turn and, briefly out of sight of his pursuers, ducks into the poorly lit entrance. He presses his heaving body against the wall and waits in the dark for the vigilante mob to pass, riled that they've lost track of their prey.

Outwitting them uplifts Mikey's self-esteem. He bounds up the stairs with aplomb, three at a time, sure of his avant-garde plan.

Big Boss is lounging on the couch in his monogrammed kimono, watching a National Geographic TV documentary about the global infestation of uncultured vultures, enhancing his pleasure with a party-sized bag of Cheetos, orange crumbs and cheesy powder everywhere.

Mikey's too focused on his mission to make a connection to all the previous Cheetos incidents.

Big Boss proffers his hand.

Mikey takes it.

But instead of the customary handshake, Big Boss tries to bite Mikey's hand.

Impulsively, Mikey recoils, not in the mood for jokes,

but immediately regrets it. Has he screwed this up already before it even started?

Mikey offers his hand back to Big Boss.

But Big Boss doesn't want it anymore, feigning hurt feelings.

To fix his faux pas, Mikey kneels and gives Big Boss a foot massage.

Big Boss closes his eyes and purrs.

Mikey notices a boner growing under the kimono.

Big Boss moans and opens his eyes. They're glistening with lust. He stands up, slowly, seductively. His belt comes loose and the kimono opens, exposing his perked up private parts in Mikey's face.

Mikey gets to his feet too and steps back.

Big Boss comes on to him.

Mikey lets him do whatever. He knows only too well how powerless we all are against our carnal desires. Plus it's his prerogative; he is the boss. Besides, Mikey wouldn't want Big Boss to think that he is close-minded, which in turn would give Big Boss an excuse to be close-minded when Mikey tells him he loves his wife.

Mikey asks where she is.

At the hospital.

Still? What's taking so long?

Mikey's flummoxed. It derails his train of thought. He's seething with jealousy. All the more urgency to divulge everything before it's too late. But he can't think straight with another man's tongue inside his mouth.

Supervisor bursts into the living room.

Big Boss peels himself off Mikey, her entrance an instant boner killer. He ties up his kimono.

Mikey pulls down his top, pulls up his shorts, and wipes his mouth, grateful for this timely interruption.

She's out of breath, wet from sweat and tears, and throws herself on the couch, convulsing in sobs.

The men inquire what's wrong.

She mumbles something unintelligible.

Big Boss offers her Cheetos; they always make him feel better.

She slaps the bag out of his hand, its contents exploding everywhere.

Big Boss is miffed. Who's going to clean it up? Him, of course, as always, and starts cleaning it up.

Mikey tries a more conventional approach, shaking the info out of her.

It only makes her cry harder.

He goes to wipe her tears, but she freaks out, doesn't want to be touched.

Big Boss yells at her to get her shit together.

It has the opposite effect. Great, now she's wailing.

He slaps her to snap out of it.

Impulsively, Mikey slaps Big Boss in her defense.

She slaps Mikey for slapping her husband.

Ok, so they all learn slapping doesn't work.

To give her space, they turn to the TV and watch a wake of rowdy vultures slurping up viscera from an antelope carcass.

Supervisor misses being the center of attention and becomes hysterical.

Big Boss loses patience and mimics her, exaggerating, showing her how ugly she looks.

Mikey concurs, she's not the prettiest of criers, but secretly, a kink in his preferences makes her that much more desirable.

Big Boss's appeal to her vanity is successful. She calms down enough to articulate a single coherent word: DEAD. It ricochets around the room.

Dead? Who's dead?

Mikey doesn't wait for the answer. He knows. Georgie has succumbed to his injuries in the hospital.

The gravitas of this revelation hits him in the chest like a wrecking ball. His muscles melt. He crumbles to the floor and releases an inhuman scream of primordial grief, like his very soul's been stabbed.

The room starts spinning. Mikey's eyes dart back and forth rapidly. He's dizzy and throws up, reduced basically to carrion not even the most uncultured vulture would find appetizing.

The protagonists of the drama on TV fly off in disgust.

Mikey's world implodes, turns impossibly black, and he free-falls through this suffocating void devoid of air.

No amount of rehearsals prepares you for the death of a loved one. It's the ultimate unimaginable. All this verbiage is garbage. Language can't express how Mikey feels.

But then a new, bleaker world erects itself around him. He doesn't recognize anything. Nothing will ever be the same. He'll have to learn to live anew, if he chooses to live at all.

He beats his guilty chest, rolls around on the ground in epic pain, grinding Cheetos into the white shag rug.

Big Boss, surprisingly, is chill about it, understanding.

He feels bad for Mikey and suggests he spend the night; their connubial bed is big enough for three.

But Supervisor, miraculously recovered, not even a trace of tears, believes that Mikey would benefit from some alone time.

Mikey hoists his saggy face and looks her in the eyes. This was their chance to finally, officially sleep together, repercussion-free.

They glare at each other.

He gets the message. She doesn't love him, perhaps never did. On top of all the other stuff, now he also feels foolish.

Mikey runs away, wanders the empty streets, woebegone.

His best friend is dead and it's his fault. The woman he loves hates him, which is also his fault, he now acquiesces.

Where are his Demons when he needs them? The assholes show up only when he doesn't.

He has no one.

He bemoans ever falling in love. Loss hurts too much to make love worth such pain. He'll never love again.

Life makes no sense. Earth is uninhabitable. If nothing mattered before, now it matters even less.

Mikey's only option is to kill himself.

He goes to the river to drown, but all he finds there is a toxic puddle too shallow to even wet his mismatched socks. His reflection in the feculent soup revolts him. He stomps on it until it's unrecognizable.

He tries a few other classic suicide recipes, but nothing works.

He's rehearsed ending his life so many times, in his head and on paper, and thought he had it all figured out, but now, when he attempts it for real, he flounders. He is totally incompetent, both at living and at dying.

Hours pass. The night is endless.

The overcast sky murmurs a rumor of a storm.

Pre-dawn, Mikey at last encounters other humans. They're involved in some suspicious activity.

He's off duty, but his professional curiosity is peaked. He hides in a shady recess of a sleeping office building, shakes off his morbid mood, and studies the scene.

Across the street, two individuals locked in a firm embrace are passionately kissing, their hands slithering around their writhing bodies, entangling each other into a complex knot only a seasoned escape artist could untie, oblivious to the rest of the world. They are practically copulating.

It's probably illegal, or should be.

Mikey is torn between wanting to exercise his patriotic duty and stop them, and satisfying his civilian libido.

He chooses to continue watching the free show, albeit still lonely as a leper and green with envy, experiencing the couple's fervent caresses vicariously, and, against his better judgment, becoming aroused.

When they inadvertently turn their profiles to him, he goes fuchsia from fright, and does his double-take.

It's Georgie and Supervisor.

Mikey must be hallucinating. He rubs his eyes, pinches his forearm, punches his thigh. No, he's never been more sober and awake.

But how is it possible?

There must be a perfectly logical explanation for this hellish vision. Either Georgie's risen from the dead, or Supervisor also died, and Mikey's watching them through some nec-romantic portal.

The third option, that she lied about Georgie's death so they can be together undercover is too devastating to even consider.

He decides to confront them and steps into a pool of streetlamp light.

Turns out he's not the only spectator of this flagrant fornication. Other Peeping Toms poke their febrile heads from behind parked cars, around corners, and out windows of surrounding buildings, all choking their engorged genitals. They look at Mikey with knitted brows and gesture to him to hide lest he spook the lovebirds before the voyeurs climax.

He ignores them. They don't know him, what he's been through.

His inner masochist watches the brazen twosome out in the open. But he finds he lacks the courage to approach or say anything.

Surely they know he's there, but couple on anyway, twisting the knife already in his back a few extra revolutions.

Stars above turn into bullets aimed directly at the bull's-eye of Mikey's heart. He flees before they kill him. As much as he wished to die before, now he's scared of death again.

While running, where or why he doesn't know, letting his legs navigate, he imagines the universe is laughing at him.

He ends up in front of Big Boss's and Supervisor's apartment, the one place on Earth he thought he'd never venture back.

Is this some cosmic joke? He turns to leave.

But then, he decides to find out if there is a secret purpose for his visit, maybe some unfinished business, or a start of a new adventure. What's the worst that can happen that hasn't already happened to him?

The door is open a crack, through which the draft whistles an eerie tune.

Mikey enters without knocking.

The door closes behind him by itself like in a horror film.

The atmosphere is tense, intense, rings of domestic violence. The air smells bad, like a bad breakup.

Mikey filters it through his hand.

Big Boss is lying unconscious or dead in a pink bubble bath. He's slit his wrists, an extreme choice for an acute hemophobe.

Mikey quickly drags him out of the tub, grabs tiny towels and ties tourniquets around his wrists, and administers First Aid, slapping him until his eyes open.

Big Boss confirms what Mikey already guessed, that his wife has left him.

To make Big Boss feel better, and prove the bitch ain't even worth it, this time for real, Mikey recounts in vivid detail everything he saw in the previous scene.

Big Boss bursts into a torrent of tears and embraces Mikey, making him cry too. They're both drowning in the same sea of sadness, and commiserate.

Big Boss pulls away first.

Mikey's hurt, but gets over it fast. This is not about him.

He dresses Big Boss in his kimono and walks him to the kitchen, sits him at the dining table.

He rummages through the cupboards for emotionally mollifying food. The bag of Cheetos is empty save for crumbs and powder. It's better than nothing.

He feeds it to Big Boss.

Big Boss doesn't want it.

It triggers Mikey's anxiety. He's been through this before with his sick Grandmother. She refused to eat, which was the beginning of the end.

He finds a box of Yogi "Smooth Your Nerves" Tea,

makes two cups, one for himself, placing the other in front of Big Boss, and sits across from him.

Mikey sips his anesthetic beverage sensually, making yummy noises, hoping to inspire his co-sufferer to do the same.

Big Boss is staring into the table, catatonic, his mind elsewhere, a hollow shell of a man.

Mikey reaches a hand toward Big Boss's mouth so he can bite it.

No reaction.

He tries to force-feed it to him, remind Big Boss how much he enjoys biting hands.

But it's as if Mikey's transparent. He almost takes it personally, almost.

They sit in strained silence for what feels like an hour although only seconds have elapsed.

Now Mikey takes Big Boss's torpid hands and nestles his face in them. They smell like a hole. If Mikey isn't careful, he may fall in. But the electric sensation caused by intimate touch of a fellow human, even without explicit consent, or especially without it, is worth everything.

Mikey's compelled to kiss Big Boss's clammy palms, and proceeds tentatively, first one, then the other.

No resistance.

Mikey nibbles on Big Boss's fingers. They taste sweet and sour.

Still no pushback.

It emboldens him to go farther. He unties the bloody towels and licks the mutilated wrists, then goes up the forearms, alternating left and right. It's just two regular guys attempting to mend their broken hearts.

But when he reaches the crook of the elbow, Big Boss's mind returns from recess, life surges back into his eyes, and he looks at Mikey as if he's the main cause of his misery. He reclaims his arms and wipes Mikey's slobber off.

Mikey's confused, doesn't know what to say. The last thing he expected was a rejection from the dude who came onto him first. Has he misread the situation, this one and the one before? How embarrassing. Red rushes into his face.

Big Boss stands up indignantly, knocking his chair over, and storms off into the bedroom.

Mikey's saliva goes rancid. He cycles through a wide range of emotions, finally settling on anger.

He races around the kitchen, lapping the table in both directions, becoming ever more inflamed.

This can't be good for his health. He stops, closes his

eyes, and tries to calm down, deep-breathing desperately, in through the nose and out through the mouth, but almost chokes on the sudden surfeit of acrid air.

He guzzles the rest of his Yogi Tea, gulps down Big Boss's untouched, unappreciated cup too, but instead of becoming smooth, his ravaged nerves erupt in fireworks.

Mikey's anger, as usual, metamorphoses into hunger. He ransacks the kitchen in search of something semi-edible to put in his mouth, finds the empty Cheetos bag, rips it apart, and voraciously licks the inside.

Cheetos, a well-known factoid, are the Devil's sustenance; the more you eat, your craving for them increases exponentially.

Mikey's beyond ravenous, and going colorblind with searing rage.

From the sink full of filthy dishes he frees a fork and a butter knife, and heads to the bedroom.

Big Boss is sitting on the edge of the bed, head in hands, rocking back and forth, whimpering woefully, a dictionary portrait of pathos.

Mikey has no pity for him, not anymore. He's done being belittled, treated like a minority, some colored foreigner. Enough.

He looks down at the keen utensils in his hands, then back up at Big Boss, and leaps like a lion, King of the Beasts, on his defenseless prey.

Big Boss lacks the motivation to fight back, making it easy for Mikey to pin him, face down in the pillow. He mounts him, and stabs his shoulder with the fork.

Big Boss's high-pitched scream, like a boiling live lobster amplified a million times, is muffled by the pillow.

All dogs in the neighborhood think they're being summoned and bark in cacophonous chorus.

Mikey saws Big Boss's meat with the butter knife. But it's too dull for the job; he makes a mess, blood splurting everywhere. This is the most frustrating dining experience Mikey's ever had. He gives up on the useless utensils, throws them away, and goes at the shoulder the old-fashioned way, with his teeth.

This is not unnatural, not at all; it happens in nature all the time. Civilization's come full circle; its end has met its origin. We're finally living out our true destiny.

But like an antelope that knows what's up when her flimsy neck's inside a lion's jaw, Big Boss pools his strength and, in a last-ditch effort, fights for his life.

Mikey does a crocodilian death-roll on him.

They mess up the bedding, rip pillows, loose goose feathers flying free. Too bad they can't take time out to appreciate the visual poetry of this indoor storm. Beauty is a luxury when it comes to sheer survival. But no way is Mikey's meal getting away from him tonight.

But then, there is an incongruous loud sound, something mechanical over their organic grunts, and from some cosmic surround-sound speakers, a song starts playing.

They freeze in a suggestive pose and swivel their heads in all directions towards the music.

It's Mikey's favorite song, "Someone Like You" by Adele.

He dismounts his dinner.

Big Boss rolls over on his back. This also happens to be his favorite song.

It means that they have everything in common and could have been best friends had their lives crossed paths earlier and under better circumstances.

Mikey lies down next to Big Boss.

The poignant song turns their hearts into warm sauce Bolognese.

The irony that his head is on Supervisor's deplumed pillow isn't lost on Mikey. But her scent, oh so sweet before, has now turned tart. He's over her, done for good, free at last.

The men lie still, holding hands, in a reverie of feather-flakes gently falling on their beleaguered bodies, and tears of joy, of relief, are rolling down their achy temples, soothing them. The song plays over and over, answering all their questions, and in the end, they cry themselves to sleep, dreamless and deep.

End of Act One.

ACT TWO

Mikey wakes up in his own apartment. He has no memory of coming home. Acidic aroma punches him in the nose.

He scans the room.

There's vomit and feces everywhere, including on walls and ceiling, plus chunks of part-digested meat and some noxious gray-green jello substance, as after an exorcism.

He feels hungover, which is odd because he doesn't drink. It's not the horrible sensation he remembers from his alcoholic days, but actually kind of relaxing, all edges softer, his old anxieties non-existent. His past seems like a nightmare and he's relieved it's over, like he's woken up into his authentic self, born-again and ready for a fresh beginning, fearless and fearsome, the exact opposite of who he's been. No more insecurities, no self-doubt, but boundless confidence and a budding clarity of purpose. He knows he can do anything he puts his mind to.

The first thing he does is clean up the apartment, a chore he used to dread, but which now is a legit joy. He whistles along with the uptempo tune in his head.

A host of Guardian Angels in gay attire, perhaps his Personal Demons transfigured, assist him in the massive task.

When later he arrives at work, everyone is terribly upset, either weeping or mad, beseeching God or cursing Him.

Mikey learns that allegedly someone ate Big Boss. All they found were his bones, a party-pack of used prophylactics, and two empty bottles of hot sauce.

A dim memory of last night's events flashes before him, but he promptly shoos it away.

His old self would have already confessed even to crimes he couldn't have possibly committed, but the new and improved Mikey is much too smart, DNA evidence notwithstanding, to admit involvement.

He doesn't feel guilty, and to his surprise, wouldn't know how even if he were. Guilt? Huh? What's guilt? As though his mental hard drive has been scrubbed of useless human hangups such as guilt.

He doesn't owe the world a thing. Au contraire, the world should apologize to him for all the unfair abuse he's had to endure.

But he acts distraught, disconsolate, rubbing his eyes to make them bloodshot. His unflagging devotion to the Cult of Stanislavsky is finally paying off, and with dividends.

He's able to produce real tears, using as catalyst the memory of his Grandmother dying in his arms.

The grieving process turns into a powerful one-man show. Mikey gives a bravura tour de force performance heavy on bathos, out-lamenting them all.

The rest of the guards feel inadequate. They watch him with admiration and respect.

Mikey is so sure of himself, on the cusp of cocky, that he even declares Big Boss's death was his fault.

No one takes him literally, which he knew would happen. They're all guilty in their own ways, and haggle over who is more to blame, each making an inventory of what they could have done or didn't do to foil their leader's gory end.

Mikey breaks up the fray before it escalates into a full-on fight, takes charge of the rowdy crowd, and restores order.

He assumes supreme authority and absolves everyone. Whatever happened happened, no way to make it unhappen, so why dwell on it?

Big Boss's death has created a power vacuum. His widow, the logical successor, is nowhere to be found. The Agency is leaderless, it's future iffy. The guards need someone they trust to tell them what to do.

They turn to Mikey. No one knows why, but they trust him implicitly.

He is ready to step into bigger shoes, and when someone hands him an actual pair of former boss's stylish shoes, and Mikey puts them on, they fit perfectly.

They elect him the new Big Boss. The vote is unanimous, almost.

Only Mikey's nemesis the Janitor strongly objects, and offers himself as a better alternative.

The others make him feel irrelevant by joking about his off-off-white social status and halal haircut.

Mikey's schadenfreude is off the chain, but he funnels it into a barely noticeable snigger. If this is not poetic justice, then poetic justice is a myth.

Janitor withdraws to sulk in the broom closet with his inanimate constituency, the cleaning supplies.

The guards encircle Mikey and ask if he agrees to be their new boss.

He demurs at first, acts coy, but when they start considering other candidates, and just as they're about to revote, he hastily accepts, under one condition, that his official title be President.

No problem. They congratulate him and, unprompted, swear an oath of loyalty.

Mikey's glowing like a pregnant woman, and he is pregnant, ready to give birth to a new self. He senses he has superpowers, just doesn't know yet what they are, but is looking forward to finding out. He acts political and adlibs a quasi-rousing speech full of threadbare third-hand statements and bloated promises, but his animated delivery is so convincing that they applaud fanatically his every word.

The first thing Mikey does as President is order his predecessor's remains, along with all the evidence, immediately cremated, claiming that a protracted investigation could, you never know, uncover information that would besmirch the martyr's memory and tarnish his widow's character.

But speaking of the widow, Supervisor finally shows up. She's disheveled, after an all-nighter of debauchery, Mikey imagines. He is happy, however, to discover that it doesn't affect him on any level.

They inform her in gruesome detail about everything that befell her husband.

She disintegrates into a writhing mass of genuine hysterics.

Everyone feels awful for her, wishes they could do something, but have their own problems to deal with.

Mikey makes a casual remark that casts a shadow of suspicion on the Supervisor. He can't say for sure that she is responsible for her husband's death, but he also can't say for sure that she isn't. He doesn't go into details, just muddies the water, and leaves the issue open for interpretation.

Supervisor is too busy rolling on the ground, blubbering insanely, to defend herself.

In this state she's useless to the Agency. But instead of terminating her employment, to demonstrate his charitable disposition, Mikey merely demotes her to Janitor's Associate, lower in rank and seniority than even his arsenal of mangy mops. It's for her own good, Mikey proclaims, so she can grieve at her own pace without serious responsibilities and worrying where her next paycheck's coming from.

The guards are moved by Mikey's gracious gesture.

He fires Georgie in absentia, giving no reasons. But he can do that now, act unreasonably, a presidential privilege. No one questions him.

He moves into his ex's and her deceased husband's spacious apartment, while magnanimously allowing her to live in his old haunted home, just for a few days, until she finds her own place.

At the reception to celebrate his inauguration, to which the Janitor and his Associate are not invited—they'd just be party-poopers—there is an employee showcase. Everyone, all one-time artists, dusts off his or her talent and performs an homage to the new commander-in-chief. There is dancing, singing, dramatic scenes and monologues from famous plays, sketch comedy improv, and a stand-up routine with benign roasting of the man of the hour. Mikey laughs convincingly. He wants them to think he's cool and has a sense of humor, though some of the jokes at his expense do hurt; he files the has-been comic's name away in his mental reminders for later. And last but not least, there is a contest of who can paint the prettiest portrait or sculpt the best bust of Mikey.

Afterwards, hard-pressed to choose the winner, in love with every entry for different reasons, he displays them all throughout his new abode.

The bacchanal concludes with each employee expressing how much they appreciate already Mikey's style of leadership, and how blessed they are to work for him.

He solicits specifics.

They go around and list the reasons why he is the

greatest President the Agency has ever had. It is ambrosia to his ears. The leave-taking becomes a soft-core orgy of one-way adulation.

Finally alone and free to unwind, Mikey reflects at leisure on his amazing fortune with a sated smile.

He puts away the pricey gourmet meats his faithful staff brought as housewarming oblations. His new palatial fridge is bursting with leftovers. If he wanted to, he could stay home a month and want for nothing. It's tempting, but there is probably work to do.

He draws a bubble-bath, dumping in double the suggested dose of the ultra-fancy bubbles imported from France, the same in which the old boss tried to kill himself, but this only adds a perverse edge to Mikey's pleasure.

He undresses, shoehorns himself in the tub, and thoroughly relaxes into his new existence, making a promise to from now spare no expense on pampering himself. Only if he is truly happy can he make others happy.

Even his rooster is excited, much bigger than Mikey remembers it ever being. His libido, not for sex per se, but for life in general, is back.

After his ablutions he lubes his pruny folds of skin with

medicated luxury Laotian lotion and feels alright alright alright; no more undignified chafing for Mikey.

He tries on Big Boss's kimono, and magically, like the shoes, it fits perfectly, even though they're dramatically different body-type and size. He changes the monogram to M for Mikey and above it sews on a patch that says PREZ.

He reclines on the couch and finds an unopened jumbo bag of Cheetos. He doesn't remember it being there before. But certain mysteries lose their luster once they're solved, so he chooses not to wonder where it came from. He opens the bag, grabs a brimming handful, and turns on the TV.

There's a show about the mating habits of hyenas on the National Geographic Channel. It's inspiring. He contemplates masturbating, but is too tired, though pleasantly. Still, he learns a lot, techniques he'll be able to use later.

He begins nodding off. Never a great sleeper, he now finds he could, if he wished to, fall asleep with ease and soundly.

But he fights to stay awake so he can bask in the positive emotions while they're fresh. Everything about his new situation, the commodious apartment with golden accents, the silk kimono, supersized Cheetos, paintings and statues of him all around, the special lotion and expensive bubbles, and so forth, all of it feels positively presidential. This must be ultimate happiness. And what a moving rags-to-riches story of which Mikey is the protagonist.

If only Grandmother could see him. Who's the fat-spawn-of-a-whore now? Huh? Who?! This goes to prove you just don't know, and never should you underestimate an individual; some can be late bloomers. She would be proud of him, he's sure, although she wouldn't express it so explicitly. In any case, he is proud and gives himself a mental pat on the back.

Thoughts of his Grandmother inevitably conjure a remembrance of the Devil. Mikey wouldn't mind his company right now; the Devil was the only one who was there for him when he was down and out. The Devil's absence during this auspicious time in Mikey's life is slightly disconcerting, but he doesn't brood over it.

It's also perfectly ok to be alone, no need to perform for anyone, just be himself, at peace, think and feel whatever comes, which for a change is all good.

Mikey's Guardian Angels stop by. They're out of breath and carelessly costumed, like they forgot their appointment and dressed in haste, their original demon garb clearly showing underneath.

Mikey gives them the most cursory of glances, sees right through them, and turns back to the bloody copulating hyenas on TV.

The demonic Angels, or, as the case may be, angelic Demons, appear shy, almost scared of Mikey. After a few awkward beats of standing around, they become self-conscious about their artsy-craftsy kindergarten pageant angel attire and take it off.

Without looking at them, Mikey rolls his eyes, sighs, and shakes his head.

They feel pointless and apologize for intruding, just came to say hi and congratulations.

Mikey doesn't need them anymore, in any guise, and dismisses them with a filigreed flick of a finger.

They excuse themselves, and vaporize.

Mikey spends the rest of the restless night in the throes of fevered afflatus, doing major rewrites of the Agency's Bylaws.

The first official day of his Presidency is super busy as he implements the changes.

Number one, because feet are a security guard's most treasured tool and must be cared for accordingly, Mikey designates foot-massage stations within walking distance of every post, and promptly, being a self-proclaimed podophile, demonstrates on a grateful guard the proper foot-massage technique.

Moreover, everyone's issued a brand new pair of haute couture orthopedic shoes. It's like Christmas came early this year, and Mikey revels in playing Santa, ho-ho-ho.

He has the uniforms blinged out, his own doubly so, as nothing repels bad guys more than flamboyance.

Each shift will start and end with a mass propaganda spectacle that he himself will choreograph, a patriotic militarish parade full of vivifying martial calisthenics.

He increases the number of guards defending the crucial Curtain from two to eight, sacrificing the security of some lesser posts.

He orders the Fourth Wall reinforced and fortified with electric current so high it fries the air. No one gets in or out alive.

To combat the rampant opinionoid epidemic, he abrogates all contradictions. As fun as it is to disagree and argue, everyone must stick to the pre-approved script.

He vows to punish treasonous antics as soon as they're suspected, no vacillation.

To help him do this right, he appeals to his employees to please police each other and report to him any irregularities.

They all submit without objections; if you haven't done anything wrong, you have nothing to fear, is their rationale.

His pet project will be to lead a Stanislavsky Masterclass, in lieu of Sunday School, where he'll interpret the Scriptures and explicate the kabbalistic sub-aspects of the Great Stanislavsky Method.

Saturdays, the Sabbath, are religiously days off, but everyone must still take part in extracurricular team-building barbecues, where Mikey's favorite game to play is Inverse Blindman's Bluff, in which everyone is blindfolded except for him. It's a lot of injury-prone fun.

Effective immediately, private Pleasure Breaks are banned. Expressions of erotic and or romantic desire are natural, nothing to be ashamed of, and shall be performed in public, especially if their object is Mikey.

What he demands above all from his staff, aside from the oath of loyalty they've already sworn to him, is love, pure, unconditional, capital L-U-V LUV.

To this end, though no one's asking for it, he gives everyone a ridiculously generous raise. It nearly depletes the

Agency's bank account, setting it on a sure course to bankruptcy, but if Mikey's learned anything from his trials and tribulations, and from his mistakes, it is the importance of living in the moment, for the pleasures of instant gratification.

These are just a few of the amendments Mikey makes to the operating procedures of the Agency. Most are met with approbation, some with vociferous enthusiasm, others not so much, but in general everyone's on board with Mikey's agenda, blindly trusting their democratically elected President.

Only the Janitor and his Associate dare voice dissenting views, but they've become such minor characters in this new chapter of Mikey's biography, an asterisk to a footnote, that he doesn't even notice. Nothing can harsh his high from his supreme success.

The honeymoon lasts longer than anyone would have expected. Mikey is seen as a benevolent ruler. He runs his kakistocracy like a family, with all the requisite dynamics and drama. He gives everyone a cool nickname, which fosters this familial bond, but also subtly alters the guards' personas, making them amenable to his avant-garde ideas. Working for Mikey is fun. The entire *corps de guards* performs their duties with *esprit de corps*.

Regrettably, but it's par for the course, he fires the most

recalcitrant employees, or those who simply don't look the part, but also a few who clearly don't deserve to lose their job, which he openly acknowledges, even calling them great people, but it must be done, as a precautionary measure, to send an unambiguous message that no one's safe.

But he hates being that guy.

They all sympathize and understand how incredibly hard it must be to be Mikey, they can't even imagine, and appreciate what he has to do; they sure couldn't do it.

At the same time, to show he doesn't just enjoy firing people, he rehires several questionable characters, who immediately join, they have no choice, his army of myrmidons.

In the end, Mikey is surrounded exclusively by acquiescent acolytes and fawning sycophants.

Who needs a solo friend when you can have the world? Mikey hasn't so much as thought of Georgie since banishing him from his affective jurisdiction.

No one quite understands why he continues to tolerate the Janitor and his Associate, Mikey's most vocal and practically sole opponents.

He doesn't have an explanation, only that governing is not a science; it's an artform, a genre of performance art, where intuition's of more use than cerebral knowledge or experience. "Truth," in air quotes—he's really into using air quotes now—"truth" doesn't always "live" where it "sleeps."

Huh? They don't get it. A mouth-breathing gawky pause.

Mikey makes additional emphatic air quotes but with nothing inside them, and winks.

Oh, ok, they nod, deciding to go along with him, sure he has good and cogent reasons for everything he does or asks them to do.

Sometimes, quite frequently, to mix things up and keep the job interesting, he sics the guards against each other by spreading rumors of what someone said or might have said about another, then sits back to watch the free-style fight. The only thing missing is a sloppy hotdog, carbonated beverage, and a mascot panda pelting him with t-shirts from a cannon, which all can be, and is, arranged.

Mikey is given free reign to make all his fantasies come true.

His approval rating soars to epoch-making heights despite a few actionable blunders he commits, but these only humanize him, make him more relatable.

Ultimately, what matters most is that the Client is satisfied, and he seems to be, exceedingly so. Often he's seen sauntering jauntily around his Property, snickering into his hands.

Since Mikey's rise to power, there have been zero threats made or attacks attempted on the treasured Curtain, and the purported mystery it may or may not be concealing remains intact.

The Client feels both safe and sufficiently entertained, finally getting his money's worth.

A few weeks into his incumbency, during a covert inspection of his dominion, Mikey spies on a group of gossiping guards. He can't hear what they're saying, but thanks to his hyperactive imagination he assumes it's all about him. When he steals too close to them, they notice him and disperse, leaving him feeling insecure.

This pesky amoeba of insecurity that nobody truly loves him quickly matures into paranoia that everybody secretly hates him, and so on his birthday, he decides to test the sincerity of his staff's affection for him.

He throws a party. Everyone except the custodial contingent is invited. But as part of the experiment, Mikey makes attendance optional, and in his hand-written, individually hand-delivered invitations he goes overboard to overstress this point. He wants to see who will show up if they really believe they don't have to.

The day of the fête, he titivates every square inch of his apartment, decorating even the decorations, colorful streamers and scented candles everywhere, and at the entrance erects a rainbow arch of balloons that spell HAPPY BIRTHDAY.

He scrapes the bottom of the Agency's coffers and curates a fifteen-course feast. He bakes a bunch of batches of caramelized bacon cookies, his Grandmother's recipe. He lays out lavish meat spreads, slow-cooked as well as tartare, exotic jerky samplers imported from around the globe, and other fun yumyums, a virtual puddingstone of alimentary marvels, everything served à la mode.

He waits. To pass the time, he watches TV and absent-mindedly snacks on the hors d'oeuvers intended for his guests.

Hours later, eyes sore and mind numb from two full seasons of a series on carnivorous flora, having eaten everything he's prepared, Mikey gives up hope that anyone will come. It is sad.

He remembers his old humdrum life and fears he'll have

to live it again. An all-but-forgotten, all-too-familiar feeling of loneliness flashfloods his soul.

No amount of anthropomorphizing of objects around him can squelch his perennial feeling of abandonment.

Hellacious heartburn, which Mikey's gotten used to living without, returns with a fanfare in full force.

Mikey can't deal. He must get this farrago of harrowing feelings off his chest fast. He's worked too hard to reinvent himself to let his new life go goodbye so easily.

In a panic, even though it's the dead of night, he decides to call an emergency staff meeting, and starts composing a mass SMS message to everyone in his contacts.

Mid-typing, he finds himself surrounded by his Personal Demons, not even a germ of the angelic about them, having fully reverted back to their original diabolical nature.

As they didn't get a chance to explore the apartment the first time they came, they take a tour, love what they see, and make themselves at home.

They eat leftover bones, lick hot and barbecue sauce off china and utensils, wrap themselves in streamers, play with candles, almost setting the couch on fire, pop a few balloons and release the rest, and draw crayon stick figures sodomizing one another into Mikey's heirloom Stanislavsky Bible.

He's out of willpower to stop them. He is exhausted and drags himself to bed.

The impudent Demons follow him to the bedroom. They start stretching and lubricating for an all-night orgy, laying out and inspecting their toys and tools, and helping one another with boners.

Mikey wants his Grandmother.

When they're good to go and jump in bed with him, however, they realize someone's already beat them to it.

As before, the Devil comes out from beneath the sheets.

Demons hiss and scurry.

Mikey sits up against the headboard, the Devil beside him, looking nothing at all like his Grandmother.

Still, Mikey's hopeful, expecting the nice Devil to make him feel better, remind him like last time what a good person he is.

Instead, the unimpeachable Prince of Darkness questions Mikey's moral code.

Mikey defends himself, playing the victim.

The Devil laughs at his pathetic jeremiad. He knows exactly who did what.

Mikey's befuddled, then quickly claims it wasn't him, whatever the Devil is referring to, but some doppelganger trying to discredit Mikey and depose him. It's a conspiracy. A witch-hunt!

The Devil isn't buying Mikey's fairytale.

Now Mikey's desperate to sell his soul, it's become a burden, and he bargains with the evil Devil.

It only provokes a scoffing cough.

Mikey couldn't give his soul away for free, or even pay the Devil to take it, that's how damaged it must be.

The Devil, in one fell sanctimonious swoop, dismantles the entire scaffolding of Mikey's core values.

Suddenly Mikey has nothing tangible to hold on to. His fastidiously fabricated character crumbles. He doesn't know who he is or who he's supposed to be, let alone who he'd like to be.

Even the portraits and statues all over the apartment, his ersatz alter egos, refuse to resemble him. Hostile strangers cackle at Mikey from canvases and pedestals everywhere he frantically turns.

He can't stay here, isn't welcome anymore, and runs out as he is, in his threadbare kimono and stupid flip-flops that seem to mock his every step with obscene suction sounds.

The Devil doesn't follow him. There is no need. Mikey

won't make it far, and then, out of options, he'll be back for more.

If his friends don't love him, maybe his enemies will, and Mikey goes back to the Church.

It's again a hectic hive of vigorous activity, a militaristic ballet class or rehearsal in progress, with all the attendant medieval torture training techniques and bondage games. Everyone's super focused and motivated. They must be prepping for something epic.

Mikey recognizes old faces, but there are also a few unfamiliar ones, probably recent recruits.

One of them looks like Georgie. What what?

Mikey's aghast. He does his signature double-take. But it's not enough, he still can't believe his eyes, so he attempts, for the first time in his career, the near-impossible, unprecedented triple-take. Semi-successfully.

But it is Georgie. This guy, the gall he has. Not only did he steal Mikey's girlfriend, but now he's going to ruin his chances of making new friends. It's bullshit!

Mikey's homicidal hatred for his XBFF tsunamies back. He's going to erupt in a hailstorm of ire unless he leaves immediately.

The goddamn Devil was right. Mikey sees no other

choice than to go home. His tormentors may still be there, but given his condition, it's better than being alone.

The apartment, however, is empty. In fact, it's full of emptiness, palpable emptiness that reeks of defeat.

The images of Mikey have also vanished. Not even these cockamamie art-brut caricatures wanted anything more to do with him.

None of the furniture makes sense, like it's been disassembled, just in from or going back to IKEA. Was the opulence counterfeit too?

The place is suffocating, nauseating, uninhabitable. The walls start spinning, the floor quaking.

Mikey's scared. He can't stand straight and lies down on the ground. In its fresh cracks he traces with a finger all the major reversals of his odyssey from spawn-of-a-whore to third-rate actor to officious prick guard to unscrupulous despot to true poltroon. His face is a palimpsest of all his failures.

He finds a piece of cheap domestic jerky, more preservatives than flesh. Food's been his only steadfast friend and panacea. He puts it in his mouth and sucks on the medicine.

But it tastes like papier-mâché, a mere prop, and he fears that nothing around him is or ever has been real, the whole world a sham set, his life a bad performance for a philistine audience.

A cloud of iridescence fills the space. Mikey's assaulted by a swarm of those translucent bloodsucking butterflies, crossbred perhaps with vampire bats, but this time there's no Georgie to shoo them away.

It's just another gratuitous moment of magic realism, minus the magic, which reality has lost a long time ago.

He retreats into the bathroom. Thinking he has to vomit, he goes down on the toilet, and dry-heaves.

He'd love to cry but can't, completely constipated.

To make himself feel better, he flees in his mind to Mexico, his safe place. It's always sunny there, the food's delicious, a mariachi band on every corner, and no one knows him. There he can be anybody, anything, be happy.

But soon, before it feels good, he's deported back to raw reality.

He has an irrepressible urge to read Georgie's Log in hope of finding himself there and takes it out from behind the toilet. He runs his thumb over the pages, and electricity shoots into his arm and spreads throughout his body.

For proper ambience, he draws a bubble bath, using

triple, maybe quadruple the prescribed amount of bubbles, drops his kimono, and stuffs himself into the tub.

He opens the Log on page one and reads. It's all there, in lapidary prose, everything Mikey and Georgie ever did together, the best of times and the worst of times. Mikey relives in fast forward their entire friendship. Even its darkest lowlights were brighter than any highlights he'd experienced before or since. Mikey and Georgie, Georgie and Mikey, affined forever, perfect for each other. What one lacked, the other had in abundance. Now Mikey would do anything to have his friend back. He'd apologize, retract everything mean he ever said or thought about him.

But it's too late. The damage is done and irreparable.

Mikey blames himself. His capacity for guilt is back, bigger than ever. He knows he deserves this abysmal quicksand of loneliness he's slowly, too slowly, sinking into, and sees no point in prolonging the pain, postponing the inevitable.

He kisses the Log goodbye and leaves it in a conspicuous place for someone to find and later publish.

He takes vanity scissors and snips the veins in his wrists, amazed, even amused, how easy it is, basic, like brushing teeth. He exhales with relief. The thought that he was ever afraid of death makes him smile. His blood mixes with hot water in the tub. He swirls the brew around. It's a literal bloodbath. Bubbles and foam turn pink, pretty, perfect as the parting image before the ultimate slow fade to black and into peaceful death.

But not so fast, because now the Ballet Bandits barge into the bathroom.

Mikey's too far gone to recognize them. He mutters some garbled gobbledygook.

They drag him out of the tub, tourniquet his wrists, and administer First Aid, slapping him into full consciousness.

Mikey brings his eyes into focus on the face above him and does a feeble double-take, more like one and a half.

It's Georgie in a revealing leopard-print unitard, his handsome ectomorph frame on full display.

Is this afterlife already where every wish comes true?

Mikey perks up and checks out the bodacious bod hovering over him.

Georgie has risen through the ranks and been promoted to Captain of the Bandits.

They're here to finally take over the lucrative gig that Mikey's Agency's been getting filthy rich on.

Actually, it's been hemorrhaging money under Mikey and is drowning in debt, but whatever, they can have it, Mikey doesn't care, and waves the whole thing off dismissively.

But it's not that simple. Evidently, while Mikey's been busy with his string of crises, Bin Janitor and his Associate have staged a coup and are now in charge.

Then what do the supercilious danseurs and danseuses want with Mikey? He's peeved. They should have let him die and deal directly with the new management.

But the Bandits need his help. Mikey has intimate knowledge of the guards, having personally brainwashed them. He knows their strengths, but above all their weaknesses, which he on purpose built into the seemingly solid infrastructure of the Agency in order to maintain total control, and just in case the Agency would need to self-destruct.

Besides, if Mikey's honest with himself, is he really cool with his archenemy the Janitor reaping the crop of his hard work and taking credit for his successes?

No, Georgie didn't think so.

And would it not be awesome to take revenge on his Associate, former Supervisor, the love of their lives, who callously broke both their hearts, and now is dating the imbecil Janitor, using him, no doubt, to regain power, but whose halal heart, once she has what she wants, she's also bound to break for sure?

Only Mikey can help the Ballet Bandits triumph over their foe. Without him they're doomed.

Mikey is flattered. He feels their sincere respect, all he's ever asked for. It's great to be needed again. If people only knew how little it takes, how easy it is to make Mikey their best friend, they'd do it more often.

Adrenalized, fresh fire in his loins, he stands up and agrees to enlist in the Bandits' noble cause.

Georgie and Mikey hug it out, keeping their pelvic areas at a professional distance. Rebuilding their personal relationship will have to wait. For now it's strictly business.

Bandits perform an abridged initiation ceremony to officially induct Mikey into the Band.

He formally receives a new war unitard and dons it over his birthday suit posthaste.

Everyone compliments him on how well it fits, even though it's very very very snug.

Captain Georgie inspects his platoon. They're battle ready. Let's rock'n'roll, girls.

They bulldoze with ease through the flawed Fourth Wall, and ambush a pair of complacent guards in front of the Curtain. Easy prey; they overpower them, then strip off their uniforms.

The rest of Mikey's ex-ensemble rushes in, stunned at seeing turncoat Mikey.

It's on, bitches, the battle of battles, unitards versus uniforms. It quickly swells to epic scope.

Mikey imitates his new confreres' paramilitary ballet moves. Turns out he's a natural, and imprecates his Grandmother for being too cheap to enroll him in ballet school. He could have been somebody.

When it appears the fight's going to be another draw, a waste of time and some lives, and there's nothing either side can do to take the lead, Mikey unleashes his trademark tornado of teeth and fingernails, mowing down the nude security guards, a freakin' blitzkrieg, but this time, his secret weapon, he also eats them, a coup de théâtre and de grâce in a single stroke.

They're powerless against his insatiable appetite for raw meat.

Seeing that it's working, the rest of the Bandits copy him, first squeamishly, but soon with fundamentalist ferocity—fresh blood is instantly addictive—turning into a maelstrom of demented whirling dervishes.

Gradually everyone's infected. The fight becomes a general all-you-can-eat gory banquet. Individuals on both sides are slaughtered and ingested, sometimes by their own, only skeletons stripped clean of flesh left littering the ground, vulgar vultures circling above incensed that there will not be leftovers.

In the end, the only survivors are Mikey, Georgie, the Janitor, and his Associate, picking meat out of their teeth with tongues, staring at one another, waiting for a sign of weakness.

Janitor blinks first.

Georgie takes advantage of this momentary lapse in concentration and murders him.

Mikey's peeved; he wanted to be the one to do it. But never mind, now Georgie has to eat him too, which Mikey wasn't looking forward to anyway.

Ex-Supervisor is a pathetic puddle of tears at the sight of her current lover's death, dismemberment, and devouring.

This only over-stimulates Mikey's salivary glands; there is nothing as delectable as a damsel in distress.

But she could be faking. Not to take any chances, Mikey jumps on her with excessive force, straddles her from behind, and, using know-how gleaned from the National Geographic Channel, sinks his incisors into the back of her neck.

She pleads for her life.

But Mikey doesn't have a soupçon of mercy for her. He licks her non-lethal wound, tenderizing the area, exhorting himself to slow down, pace himself. He always eats too fast and then gets indigestion.

Georgie, done with his main course, ready for desert, something sweet to get the awful taste of offal out of his mouth, joins them.

He burps a little undigested Janitor in her face. Pardonez moi.

Mikey is impressed with his friend's creative cruelty.

As a last resort, to inveigle them to spare her life, she employs her usual ammo, sexuality, brainstorming several salacious scenarios that involve all three of them, first verbally, but when they won't budge, she starts enacting them also physically.

It is now she who grinds on them, groping taboo body parts, faking orgasm sounds.

But all to no avail. Their hearts, the most important sexual organ, have moved on, and, both being hopeless romantics, able to engage in sex acts only when in love, their roosters remain dormant.

They get down to the business of eating her even though she's still alive, screaming, writhing in agony, going in and out of consciousness. It's the freshest meat available anywhere, the cleanest, purest pleasure imaginable. They savor every bite. There is enough of her for both of them. What was their problem before? Neither understands now. But it's water under the bridge.

They leave not a single morsel of muscle on the bones, saving the best for last, her heart. Now they know what manna from Heaven tastes like.

To wash down the meal, Mikey and Georgie drink all her blood, and she dies.

It's just the two of them in front of the Curtain, like the good old days. There is nothing better than losing all hope, giving up on a dream completely, only for it to then come true when you least expect it. Their reunion is a miracle. They've never been happier.

After licking their fingers clean, using them to comb their hair, and realigning their rumpled unitards, they lock eyes.

Best friends forever?

Best friends forever.

They embrace, their pelvises making full contact, then come apart, laugh triumphantly, and re-embrace.

For old-times sake, they reenact the greatest hit scenes of their friendship, faux-seriously performing standard security procedures, slightly exaggerated, stylized for their aesthetic enrichment, but also uninhibited horsing around, frolicking freely among the skeletal remains of the dead they've left in their wake.

They stop in front of the enigmatic Curtain and contemplate opening it, finally finding out what the big deal has been. They locate the slit in the middle and look at each other for courage.

Then bang, there is a loud explosion behind them.

They're thrown back away from the Curtain like it's electrified.

When the orange smoke clears, the Devil is standing there downstage. His gelid gaze and incongruous cunning smile hold them frozen in a twisted pose.

Mikey makes that reflex moan that people make when meeting someone they used to love but haven't yet had closure.

Georgie recalls their very first encounter with the Devil. He checks on Mikey.

Mikey shakes off his anxiety.

Then, just like before, they circumnavigate the intruder, a chance to reprise yet another crucial scene from their shared past.

When they swirl in close enough to apprehend him, the duplicitous Devil glides between them towards the Curtain. It's déjà vu.

They look stupid, worse than the first time.

The Devil takes off his mask, ta-da, revealing underneath the face of the Client.

Mikey and Georgie gawk at him slack-jawed.

The Client-Devil informs them with a smug sneer that the Property they've been guarding and fighting over, risking their disposable bogus lives, has absolutely no value. The Curtain is a worthless piece of secondhand cloth purchased in a thrift shop. There was no purpose for the drama that has taken place.

Before Mikey and Georgie can organize their thoughts and formulate follow-up questions, the preternatural protean creature explodes and with an eldritch laughter disappears inside another cloud of smoke, much thicker this time, and no longer orange, but purple, and a pungent smell of lavender lingers in the air long afterwards, while the Devil has moved on to some new other-colored mischief.

It takes Mikey and Georgie forever to recover from their asthma attack.

They come together, each making sure the other is ok.

It occurs to them that historically, when has the Devil told the truth? Why should they believe him now?

They approach the Curtain to check for themselves. Slowly, full of apprehension teetering on fear, they draw it open, revealing another, different hue and style curtain.

They open it too, this one more aggressively.

There's yet another variant of curtain.

Is this a joke? Just a sequence of curtains ad infinitum?

Their obstinacy pays off. When they pull back the third curtain, a stage is unveiled. A fecund, formless field, pregnant with possibility ...dense haze hanging in the air, celestial shafts of light.

There is that unmistakable mechanical sound already familiar to Mikey, and again from invisible cosmic speakers Adele's "Someone Like You" starts playing.

Georgie, mystified, looks at Mikey.

Is this their cue?

They smile, nod, instinctively know exactly what to do, and begin dancing in flawless unison the very number they started together, now magically finished, like they've been rehearsing all along ... and dance back into their common dream.

Blackout.

The End.

LOOKING BACK

A conversation between FLORIAN MALZACHER *and* KELLY COPPER/NTOK *on the occasion of the world premiere of* No President: A Story Ballet of Enlightenment in Two Immoral Acts.

FLORIAN MALZACHER. Nature Theater of Oklahoma—the name of your company is taken from Franz Kafka's unfinished novel *Amerika*. Why did you choose it?

KELLY COPPER. In Kafka's novel, the Nature Theatre of Oklahoma is a place of longing. The protagonist, Karl Rossmann, has been through a series of pretty lousy jobs in America when he sees a poster for the Nature Theater offering jobs for everyone. And he is hired straight away as a technician—without any experience—and soon afterwards is on a train to Oklahoma. The novel is unfinished, so we don't know how things work out for him. But to us this theatre company was always an ideal. What's more, Pavol moved from Czechoslovakia to Oklahoma when he was just eighteen, like Karl Rossmann, and had a very tough year there. For him, *Amerika* was a sort of user's manual for his life there. Because he didn't find a Nature Theatre of Oklahoma, we had to make it ourselves.

FM. For many years you've lived in New York—a city that's famous for avant-garde art. Is it sometimes difficult to work in a city with such a legacy?

KC. When I first visited New York as a student in 1992, in

one weekend I saw performances of the Wooster Group, Richard Foreman, Reza Abdoh—and a film by Jack Smith. I was blown away, and vowed to return as soon as possible. That same year I met Pavol at university—and in 1993 we moved to New York. It's a city where history, art and garbage collide. For a long time we lived across the street from the old Electric Circus, where the Velvet Underground first played. And the apartment where Jack Smith created his performances was not far away. All of that has gradually disappeared—the Electric Circus became a center for drug addicts and then later a delicatessen—but you can feel that underground art history wherever you go. It has a particular kind of vitality, a feeling that everything is possible even if it's not strictly permitted. We now live in Queens, where apparently 800 different languages are spoken. For two somehow homeless artists, it's the perfect home. We take from and are inspired by all that is around us. Even, or especially, the ugly bits. In New York—it's quite small for a big city—so you come in contact with all of it eventually.

FM. Jack Smith, who you just mentioned, had a very specific influence on your new work: *No President* was the title of his last film. Of course one automatically thinks of the political situation in the USA. But the subtitle also refers to the more European genre of the story ballet.

KC. A lot of that is linked to our interest in narrative. In a classical story ballet—such as *The Nutcracker* for example—you need to know the plot in advance to be able to read it in the dance. The first piece our company ever did was a "dance" piece with no words. We determined all the entrances and exits, and in fact all of the movement, by chance—or, to be more precise, by rolling dice. Nevertheless the audience still projected stories onto the events constantly. This time we're starting at the opposite end: there is a highly complex story, a huge amount of text and we're trying to abstract movements out of the language Narrative ballet as a genre is an important inspiration for this, which is also why we're using the music of 'The Nutcracker.' But there are also very different sources alongside that: fitness exercises, slapstick and documentaries about animal predators. So it's a rather unorthodox mix—just as Jack Smith's film is patched together, like Frankenstein's monster, out of very different materials.

FM. *No President* tells the story of a museum guard who works for a security firm that consists of former actors. And they are guarding a theatre curtain...

KC. Yes, originally the Museum of Modern Art (MoMA) invited us to make a new piece of work. In the end it didn't work out, but at the time we did a lot of thinking about museums as containers for performance, the difference between a white cube and black box and the relationship between life and art. The fact that Pavol had spent several years working as a museum guard at the Metropolitan Museum of Art also contributed. Very few people are aware that a great many of the guards in New York museums are themselves artists, painters, theatre makers and sculptors. Living (hunger) artists watch over breathtakingly expensive works by mostly dead artists. In *No President* we imagine a future in which all artists are employed as security guards. The curtain that they are guarding is kind of portal to the unknown—something that no one is allowed to see. This preoccupation with museums, money, and art is one we share with Jack Smith. In many of his performances and writings he fought for the reality of art as Art and against art as private property. He was particularly critical of museums hiding art away from the public. You could say that this is exactly what *No President* is about. There's a nice quote from Smith: "Museums give nothing. They claim to give you art and then they take it away again after two or three weeks. This is a disgusting performance when you think that art should be free. Everything should be free and it could begin with art."

FM. In the piece things soon get out of control—there's a whole lot of love, sex, and death—but also a lot of splatter and even excessive cannibalism. It's reminiscent of the early films of Christoph Schlingensief, who was also a big Jack Smith fan.

KC. For some years now there's been more and more violence in our work. Somehow almost organically we've now ended up with cannibalism. In our last theatre piece—*Pursuit of Happiness*—there's a section set in Iraq and that's quite violent. Drawing on inspiration from Grand Guignol we really pushed that as far as we could go. We're interested in the representation of violence because violence on stage always plays with the boundaries of what is possible in the theatre. At the end of *Pursuit of Happiness,* for example ,all the actors are limping, one pretends to have limbs missing and holds a marble between his fingers claiming it's his eye. We're fascinated by the discrepancy between representation and reality. Representing violence on stage necessarily requires a great many theatrical devices—and we exaggerate that. As an actor you have no chance of presenting anything as being remotely real with these ridiculous props. But you try anyway and fight against how ridiculous it is. Everybody can see how artificial it is. But it's also a bit sad. Just like us. Just like life. At the end, when the stage is filled with dead bodies, that's not an empty metaphor: it's also an expression of despair at the world we live in.

FM. But for people who aren't splatter fans you also offer points of reference to other traditions: for example, there's a pact with the Devil like in Faust. And the auctorial onstage narrator—he's the only one who speaks—is a little reminiscent of Thomas Mann's *Spirit of Storytelling* with his irony and the way he interferes in what is happening from time to time.

KC. Yes, the untrustworthy authorial narrator fits the story well. He's not outside the action, watching with indifference or even benign intent, but mixed up in it somehow. Not like a God-like omniscient, but more of a slippery, creative type.

FM. You were always interested in putting performers (and yourselves) in situations they could not easily cope with. Even in your early pieces, for example, actors had to dance and dancers had to sing. In *No President* the cast consists of actors from New York and Düsseldorf, dancers and also semi-amateurs. What interests you in this mix?

KC. What always interests us is people—and in this case their very particular relationship to dance and performance. Each one of the performers has—and for us this is more important than their level of skill—a different relationship to the physical material in the show. For some of them, dance is the centre of their life and work, for some it's modern dance, for others it's ballet. And then for some of them dance is an entirely new physical challenge—or possibly a passion that they have not yet had a chance to pursue. What matters is that for all of them, the relationship is not an indifferent but a substantial one. Many of them are working with us for the first time, while others have been part of Nature Theater of Oklahoma for many years, and we want them to bring themselves and their history on stage with them—and to share that with the audience.

FM. One of the recurrent notes you give to the actors and the extras during rehearsals is: never forget the reality around you. Always stay in contact with the audience, even eye contact.

KC. That is the key thing: the performers cannot let the audience see them without consequences. Without looking back. The actors are not objects, they are people too. The most important reality is always the primary one, which is that the performance is a gathering of people sharing space and time. Of course there are rules for this interaction—the performers sit on one side and the audience on the other—but I have always enjoyed the complexity of the actual situation more than that of the fictional one. The truth is that these guys on stage all have thoughts and feelings and questions—for themselves and for the audience. I want them to bring all that to the table along with whatever fiction we're enacting. And the truth is often in the eyes. So I want the audience to see their eyes—eyes that are looking back, as people do.

FM. It's also important not only not to make it too easy for the actors, but also not to make it too easy for the audience. This is another reason for the excessive violence: it prevents the audience just amusing themselves. At the same time this reminder of the reality outside of the fiction is rather Brechtian—a variation on the famous sign: "Don't gawp so romantically." Even though Brecht meant less the reality of the theater space than the social reality outside of the theater.

KC. Exactly. For theater to have social consequences, it cannot ignore the social dynamic of the space. Or of the rehearsal which comes with its own set of rules: the director is a kind of dictator, but I think it's important for performers not to abdicate completely. I like to see a performer execute a move perfectly, sure, but also with a little resistance. I don't want to see them lose themselves in the process. In the same way, we cultivate a little resistance from the audience too. You're not only going to have people in the audience who are enjoying themselves all the time. Hopefully there will also be people having all kinds of feelings about our show and expressing that in various ways. If we are any good, we can use whatever energy that gives to go deeper into the work at hand.

FM. *No President* is a piece about the life of a (failed) artist with all the doubts and hubris of artistic work. And it is full of references to theater discourse, quoting choreographies by Anne Teresa De Keersmaeker, for example. But the main reference point is the Russian acting theorist Konstantin Stanislavsky—why do you pick on him?

KC. I think we take a punch at Stanislavsky here because he is just (sadly) the beginning and end of all actor training in America. It's always Stanislavsky, always looking inside you for some kind of childhood trauma... focusing actors' work primarily on themselves. Whereas for me, as I've said, a very different kind is what's most important: actors' work with their fellow actors on stage and on the audience!

GLOSSARY

KAKISTOCRACY: a system of government which is run by the worst, least qualified, or most unscrupulous citizens. The word was coined as early as the seventeenth century, but gained significant use in the first decades of the twenty-first century to criticize populist governments emerging in different democracies around the world. American poet James Russell Lowell used the term in 1876, in a letter to Joel Benton, writing, "What fills me with doubt and dismay is the degradation of the moral tone. Is it or is it not a result of Democracy? Is ours a 'government of the people by the people for the people,' or a Kakistocracy rather, for the benefit of knaves at the cost of fools?" The word returned to use during the 2016 U.S. presidential campaign, particularly by opponents and critics of Republican presidential candidate Donald Trump.

LEGERDEMAIN: 1. skilful use of one's hands when performing conjuring tricks. 2. a display of skill or adroitness, 3. deception; trickery. Borrowed from French *léger de main* (literally "light (weight) of hand").

OBSEQUIOUS: obedient or attentive to an excessive or servile degree. Excessively eager and attentive to please or to obey instructions. The word comes from the Latin root *sequi*, meaning "to follow."

RECALCITRANT: having an obstinately uncooperative attitude towards authority or discipline. Not obedient or compliant; refractory. Mid-19th century: from Latin recalcitrant—

"kicking out with the heels," from the verb *recalcitrare*, based on *calx*, *calc-* "heel."

PORTENTOUS: of or like a portent; of momentous significance, giving a sign or warning that something usually bad or unpleasant is going to happen. Or: done in a pompously or overly solemn manner so as to impress.

MYRMIDON: a follower or subordinate of a powerful person, typically one who is unscrupulous or carries out orders unquestioningly. The Myrmidons were a legendary people of Greek mythology, native to the region of Thessaly. During the Trojan War, they were commanded by Achilles, as described in Homer's *Iliad*. According to Greek legend, they were created by Zeus from a colony of ants and therefore took their name from the Greek word for ant, *myrmex*.

ABSQUATULATE: leave quickly; abscond, decamp, skedaddle, vamoose; to leave abruptly, to make off with something or someone. Attested since the 1830s in American English, a jocular mock-Latin word. Blend of abscond + squat + perambulate, as ab- ("away (from)," as in abscond) + squat + -ulate (as in perambulate), hence meaning "get up (from a squat) and depart (quickly)."

SPANK-BANK: a memorable collection of mental images that one wishes to retain for masturbation purposes.

ACQUIESCENT: ready to accept something without protest, or to do what someone else wants. Early 17th century: from Latin *acquiescent*—"remaining at rest," from the verb *acquiescere* (see *acquiesce*).

PANDEMONIUM: coined by John Milton in *Paradise Lost*, Pandæmonium, from Ancient Greek παν (pân, "all") (equivalent to English pan-) + Late Latin *daemonium* ("evil spirit, demon"), from Ancient Greek δαιμων (daímōn, "deity"). 1. (archaic) a place where all demons live; Hell. 2. chaos; tumultuous or lawless violence. 3. an outburst; loud, riotous uproar, especially of a crowd.

VOCIFEROUS: expressing or characterized by vehement opinions; loud and forceful. Vociferous derives from the word Latin *vox*, which means "voice." But other English words can be used to describe those who compel attention by being loud and insistent. "Vociferous" implies a vehement shouting or calling out, but to convey the insistency of a demand or protest.

ADULATION: excessive admiration, praise, or flattery. From the Latin verb *adulari*, meaning "to fawn on" (a sense used specifically of the affectionate behavior of dogs) or "to flatter."

AFFLATUS: a divine creative impulse or inspiration. Mid-17th century: from the Latin verb *afflare*, from *ad-* "to" + *flare* "to blow." A term that was derived from Cicero in *De Natura Deorum* ("The Nature of the Gods"), it can be taken to mean "to be blown upon" by a divine wind, like its English equivalent *inspiration*, which comes from *inspire*, meaning "to breathe/blow onto."

POLTROON: a spiritless coward. Early 16th century: from French *poltron*, from Italian *poltrone*, perhaps from *poltro*, meaning "sluggard."

MOSH PIT: punching, kicking, and generally being violent to

live music. An area in front of a stage where very physical and rough dancing takes place. Moshing or slamdancing is a style of dance in which participants push or slam into each other, typically performed in "aggressive" live music. Moshing usually happens in the center of the crowd, generally closer to the stage, in an area called the "pit" (sometimes called a "mosh pit"). It is intended to be energetic and full of body contact.

SCHADENFREUDE: a compound of *schaden* "damage, harm" and *freude* "joy." "Harm-joy" is the experience of pleasure, joy, or self-satisfaction that comes from learning of or witnessing the troubles, failures, or humiliation of another. A pleasure derived by someone from another person's misfortune.

CALISTHENICS: gymnastic exercises to achieve bodily fitness and grace of movement. Derives from the ancient Greek words *kallos* (καλλος), which means "perfect" or "good" (to emphasize the aesthetic pleasure that derives from the perfection of the human body), and *sthenos* (σθενος), meaning "strength" (great mental strength, courage, and determination). It is the art of using one's bodyweight as resistance in order to develop physique. Examples of calisthenic exercises are push-ups, burpies, handstands, squats, leg raises, planks and shuttle runs.

JURISDICTION: the practical authority granted to a legal body to administer justice within a defined field of responsibility. From the Latin *ius*, *iuris* meaning "law" and *dicere* meaning "to speak." Power or right of a legal or political agency to exercise its authority over a person, subject matter, or territory.

SYCOPHANT: a servile self-seeking flatterer, a person who acts obsequiously towards someone important in order to gain advantage. From the mid-16th century (denoting an informer): from French *sycophante*, or via Latin from Greek *sukophantēs*, "informer."

ANTHROPOMORPHIZE: to attribute human form or personality to things not human.

AIR QUOTES: a pair of quotation marks gestured by a speaker's fingers in the air, to indicate that what is being said is ironic or mocking, or is not a turn of phrase the speaker would typically employ.

NATURE THEATER OF OKLAHOMA

> "Personnel is being hired for the Theater in Oklahoma! The Great Nature Theater of Oklahoma is calling you! It's calling you today only! If you miss this opportunity, there will never be another! Anyone thinking of his future, your place is with us! All welcome! Anyone who wants to be an artist, step forward! We are the theater that has a place for everyone, everyone in his place! If you decide to join us, we congratulate you here and now! But hurry, be sure not to miss the midnight deadline! We shut down at midnight, never to reopen! Accursed be anyone who doesn't believe us!"
>
> —Franz Kafka, *Amerika*

Nature Theater of Oklahoma is an award-winning New York art and performance enterprise under the direction of Pavol Liška and Kelly Copper. With each new project, we attempt to set an impossible challenge for ourselves, the audience, and our collaborators—working from inside the codes and confines of establishe genres and exploding them. No two projects are formally the same, but the work is always full of humor, earnestness, rigor, and the audience plays an essential role—whether as spectators, or, just as often, as participants in the work.

Using readymade material, found space, gifted properties, cosmic accident, extreme formal manipulation and plain hard work, Nature Theater of Oklahoma makes art to affect a shift in the perception of everyday reality that extends beyond the site of performance and into the world in which we live.

53rd State Press publishes new writing for performance. Our catalog includes plays as well as scores and notations for interdisciplinary performance, graphic adaptations, and essays on theater and dance. 53rd State Press was founded in 2007 by Karinne Keithley. In 2017, Kate Kremer took on the leadership of the volunteer editorial collective. For more information or to order books, please visit 53rdstatepress.org.

53rd State Press books are represented to the trade by TCG (Theatre Communications Group). TCG books are exclusively distributed to the book trade by Consortium Book Sales and Distribution, an Ingram Brand.

No President is made possible by the New York State Council on the Arts with the support of the Office of the Governor and the New York State Legislature.

NEW YORK STATE OF OPPORTUNITY. | Council on the Arts

53rd State Press
new writing for performance